HANDBOOK AND CATALOG FOR INSTRUCTIONAL MEDIA SELECTION

HANDBOOK AND CATALOG FOR INSTRUCTIONAL MEDIA SELECTION

BRIAN G. BOUCHER, MERRILL J. GOTTLIEB AND MARTIN L. MORGANLANDER

EDUCATIONAL TECHNOLOGY PUBLICATIONS
ENGLEWOOD CLIFFS, NEW JERSEY 07632

Library of Congress Cataloging in Publication Data

Boucher, Brian G
   Handbook and catalog for instructional media selection.

   Includes bibliographical references.
   1. Teaching—Aids and devices—Catalogs. 2. Audio-visual education—Handbooks, manuals, etc. I. Gottlieb, Merrill J., joint author. II. Morganlander, Martin L., joint author. III. Title.
LB1043.Z9B68   371.3   72-11983
ISBN 0-87778-045-5

Copyright © 1973 Educational Technology Publications, Inc., Englewood Cliffs, New Jersey 07632.

Printed in the United States of America.

Library of Congress Catalog Card Number: 72-11983.

International Standard Book Number: 0-87778-045-5.

First Printing: January, 1973.

Foreword

This book is the result of an extensive reevaluation of a systematic approach to media selection originally developed by the authors for the Grumman Aerospace Corporation under contract to the U.S. Navy. The system was first applied in the design of enlisted personnel maintenance training on the F-14 "Tomcat" fighter aircraft. As a result of that experience and various pilot studies of the use of the system with more academic subject areas, there has been an extensive reorientation of the portion concerned with instructional strategy and learner activity. The book also reflects the results of continuing investigation of commercially available instructional devices which have come on the market since the original study was produced for the Navy.

The system itself dates back to 1967 when the senior author, along with several representatives of the industrial and educational communities, began work on a matrix approach to instructional media selection as the Media Task Group of Project ARISTOTLE. In the succeeding years this basic approach has been followed by various researchers and authors for military, industrial, and educational applications. The approach, however, has not been without problems. Attempts at a simple yes-no rating of generic media types regarding suitability to satisfy particular learning objective requirements have been especially subject to fluctuation. It would appear that as fast as a set of yes-no ratings were developed, new technological developments immediately required that the ratings be changed. Rating scales such as poor-fair-good have been considered as too subjective, engendering more argumentation than application. In general, these ratings have primarily addressed the capabilities of various generic media to satisfy the presentation requirements of particular objectives with little or no attention to various instructional strategies and learner behaviors. They have, however, made substantial progress toward developing a definitive taxonomy of presentation requirements.

The selection system described in this book attempts a more empirical than subjective evaluation of the various generic media with indications of suitability being based on investigation of commercially available devices rather than reflecting any pre-defined conception of a generic media type.

In investigating the thousands of instructional devices available, the authors have received the cooperation and support of manufacturers and their distributors in making information and the devices themselves available for evaluation. A number of users of these devices, including military establishments, industrial concerns, schools, and colleges also gave most willingly of their time and their assistance. Particular credit is due to the many people in both the U.S. Navy and the Grumman Corporation who had the foresight to permit this project to be approached with a view to its wider application beyond the needs of military technical training. Specific recognition must be given to Hector W. Hill and Alfred T. Mazza of the Grumman Corporation for their contributions to the manuscript.

Usage

The media selection system and descriptive data in this book are designed to assist media specialists, curriculum designers, and teachers to arrive at informed decisions regarding the use of currently available educational hardware. It presents a step-by-step process of analyzing learning objectives, determining appropriate generic media types, and selecting specific instructional devices to aid in meeting those objectives. It is not, nor is it intended to be, a fully automatic process. It is, rather, an attempt to add the results of several years of research and experience with educational hardware to the knowledge of subject matter and educational technique provided by the user. It does this by first providing a common language so that potential technological solutions can be systematically matched and tested against educational problems. It provides information regarding the constraints on these matches. Finally, it provides standardized descriptions of individual devices to permit identification of specific makes and models of equipment which will satisfy the user's requirements.

Earlier versions of this work have been utilized in a number of different ways. Fully developed learning objectives have been processed by training specialists in the design of large scale technical/vocational training programs. In other cases, devices have been identified by computer which meet predetermined specifications. The most fruitful utilization, however, has occurred when the system has been integrated with the generation of specific learning objectives.

Integrating media selection with the development of objectives provides maximum flexibility in determining both the "condition" and "behavior" elements of the objective.* The various presentation, interaction, and strategy parameters which are listed on the Media Requirements Worksheet (described in Chapter 1) have proved to be stimulating to the design of objectives as well as descriptive of the final result.

Integrating the two processes also permits early realization (and corrective action, if necessary) of the economic and logistical implications of a particular objective statement. Generally, the selection system will yield a number of different generic media candidates for each objective. An essential part of the final media selection is the comparison of the lists of candidate media for each objective to find a reasonable mix which takes maximum economic advantage of the commonality

*The two-way interaction of media and objectives is addressed in Chapter 5 of Gronlund (1971).

among the lists. When a trend is seen among most objectives in a set, it may be possible to adjust the requirements of the remaining ones to minimize expense and diversity. Available software is also a frequent and sometimes overriding consideration. Where feasible, more than one approach to an objective using different media can provide for an *adaptive* capability not inherent in a single medium.*

Brian G. Boucher
Merrill J. Gottlieb
Martin L. Morganlander

*The reader is directed to the outstanding work of Dr. Joseph E. Hill and his associates at Oakland Community College in Bloomfield Hills, Michigan for information regarding the matching of alternative presentation media to the cognitive style of students.

Table of Contents

PART III—SPECIFIC DEVICE SELECTION

List of Figures

HANDBOOK AND CATALOG FOR INSTRUCTIONAL MEDIA SELECTION

PART ONE
GENERIC MEDIA SELECTION

1

Analysis of Objectives

In order to determine appropriate media for the accomplishment of specific learning objectives, it is first necessary to analyze the objectives to determine the information to be provided the learner and the behavior expected of him.

This information is further analyzed with regard to the sense modality desired for the presentation of the material to be learned (Visual, Auditory, Tactile, Kinesthetic, or combinations thereof) and various subcategories such as motion, color, dimensionality, texture, etc. Desired learner behavior is then analyzed with regard to the modality of response (performance, or verbal/symbolic) and various subcategories such as indication, recognition, manipulation, gross body movements, etc. Finally, the instructional strategy is analyzed with regard to type of feedback to the learner and type of interaction with the learner. The worksheet for use in this analysis is shown in Figure 1. For each objective, the applicable requirements are checked, thus giving a *Requirements Profile* of that objective for later use in the system. (This worksheet may be duplicated by the reader for noncommercial, instructional purposes.)

The specific definitions of the parameters as used in the worksheet are as follows:

Presentation Parameters

Visual

Plane (2D). Material can be presented in two dimensions such as by print, drawings or photographs including two dimensional representations of three dimensional objects.

Solid (3D). Material requires direct perception of three dimensionality. This presumes the ability to shift the viewing point and perceive aspect changes.

Locality (3D). A special case of three dimensionality in which the viewing point is inside the material. This presumes the ability to locate material above and below, in front and in back, and to the sides of the observer.

Motion, Full. Material requires perception of changes in relative position of viewed objects. Full motion presumes the ability to follow an object through all movements including changes in position, relationship, and place.

Motion, Cyclical. Material requires perception of simple repeated changes in relative positions or relationships of viewed objects without requiring changes in place. Included in this category are flow illusions where cyclical changes in portions of the material create the illusion of continuous movement through the material.

Motion, Limited Excursion. Material requires perception of the movement of a simple element within the visual image, such as the movement of a spot light or pointer.

Motion, Conceptual. Material requires perception of activity within the visual field to suggest motion or other time-related changes such as flashing on and off, sample images from a continuing sequence, etc.

Color. Material requires perception of differences in hue and saturation.

Auditory

Quality. Material requires perception of differences in pitch, loudness, and timbre.

Locality. The auditory equivalent of visual locality (see above).

Tactile

Size/Shape/Texture. Material requires perception of size, shape, or texture through the sense of touch.

Temperature. Material requires perception of temperature of objects or environment.

Motion. Material requires tactile perception of physical movements.

Kinesthetic Cues

Material requires perception of positions, motions, and accelerations through sense organs inside the body.

MEDIA REQUIREMENTS WORKSHEET	PRESENTATION																STUDENT RESPONSE								INSTRUCTIONAL STRATEGY							
	VISUAL								AUDI-TORY		TACTILE					VERBAL/SYMBOLIC			PER-FORMANCE			FEEDBACK			INTERACTION						
	PLANE (2D)	SOLID (3D)	LOCALITY (3D)	MOTION, FULL	MOTION, CYCLICAL	MOTION, LTD. EXCUR.	MOTION, CONCEPTUAL	COLOR	QUALITY	LOCALITY	SIZE/SHAPE/TEXTURE	TEMPERATURE	MOTION	KINESTHETIC CUES	SELECTION	SPECIFIC	CREATED	INDICATION	MANIPULATION	GROSS BODY MOVEMENT	INFORMATIVE	EVALUATIVE	CORRECTIVE	LINEAR	BRANCHING	ADAPTIVE	REPETITIVE

Student Response Parameters

Verbal/Symbolic

Responses which are expressed in words, symbols, diagrams, pictorials, etc.

Selection. A recognition task which requires selection of a correct response from a group of alternatives presented to the learner. This can be "multiple-choice," matching or true/false type responses.

Specific. A recall task which requires the learner to construct a specific or particular response.

Created. A recall task which requires the learner to construct a response using his own choice of words, illustration, etc.

Performance

Responses which are expressed by actual performance of a sensory-motor skill.

Indication. A recognition task which requires the learner to signify the location of physical objects by pointing.

Manipulation. A performance task which is limited to manual skills.

Gross Body Movement. A performance task involving use of the limbs or in which the environmental context is essential to the task.

Instructional Strategy Parameters

Feedback

The type of information immediately available to the learner regarding his responses.

Informative. The learner is informed of the correct response without regard to how or if the learner actually responded.

Evaluative. Feedback is given to the learner indicating whether or not the learner's response was correct.

Corrective. The learner is provided with specific commentary on the response particularly concerning what was wrong with an incorrect response.

Interaction

Strategies which require a two-way communication between the learner and the material, that is to say that the presentation of material is affected by learner behavior.

Linear. Presentation rate is learner controlled. A fixed sequence of instructional units is presented one at a time with mastery of one unit being a precondition of presentation of the next unit in the sequence.

Branching. Presentation sequence and rate is learner controlled. Material includes alternative units which are presented as a result of student responses indicative of incorrect or incomplete understanding of previously presented material.

Adaptive. Instructional strategy itself can be varied as a result of both current and past learner behavior.

Repetitive. The learner can easily cause a desired portion of the presentation to be repeated. Unlike the other types of interaction which depend on the learner's responses, Repetitive Interaction can take place at the learner's volition.

2

Media Capabilities Matrix

The Media Capabilities Matrix (Figure 2) is a detailed exposition of the capability of various generic media types and some unique devices to satisfy requirements for each of the parameters used in the learning objective analysis. The list of media itself must be somewhat arbitrary. For example, in the television area the matrix includes separate evaluations for video recording, live television, and slow scan television (SSTV). The distinction between video recording and live TV is based on the issue of real-time vs. storage, with the resulting difference in the ability to repeat and review material (*repetitive interaction*). The distinction between SSTV and video recording is based on the comparative ability to present full visual motion. Suggestions that video cassette recording is itself a unique medium have been rejected on the basis that it could not be differentiated from reel-to-reel video recording by its ratings in the matrix. Similarly, "single concept film loops" are not differentiated from other motion pictures in terms of matrix ratings. This does not deny the obvious differences in convenience, but this is a *quantitative* difference, whereas the matrix is concerned only with *qualitative* distinctions. Perhaps the most remarkable omission from the generic media listing is the human instructor.* The omission signifies neither oversight nor undervaluation. Rather, the assumption has been made that the human instructor is an essential element of *all* media, at least in the planning and programming phases. Where the instructor is a necessary part of the presentation, response, and/or strategy phases, that necessity is noted in the ratings themselves.

The media listing is comprised of three sections. The first contains media generally consisting of more-or-less standard hardware (if any is required) with software specific to the subject matter. This hardware is further analyzed in the later chapters of this book. The second section includes unique devices which do not fit in any of the generic categories of the first section, or which make such unusual

---

*At the second annual Educational Technology Conference in New York in March, 1972, it was suggested that separate listings be made for teachers, paraprofessionals, and resource persons.

usage of the software normally associated with first-section media as to require a separate listing for adequate exposition. The third section contains media where the hardware itself is either specifically designed for the subject matter or where it is usually custom-designed for each individual installation. In this latter category, the matrix omits systems which are simple multiples of media in the first section, such as dial-access audio systems, language laboratories, multi-channel television distribution systems, etc.

The ratings within the matrix are intended to indicate the suitability (or lack thereof) of each medium to meet each parameter. Often, this suitability is a function of how the medium is used, so that a number of symbols have been included to indicate various accessories or other utilization factors. The services of an instructor are one such factor which occasionally is the only means whereby a medium can satisfy a particular requirement. When such is the case, it is indicated in the ratings. There are many other cases, however, when an instructor can substitute for another accessory or utilization factor. For example, the instructor can point to a portion of any visual image (MOTION, Limited Excursion), or provide a narration to go with an image (AUDITORY: Quality). However, these do not cover the full range of possible requirements of these two parameters. Thus, for these two parameters, preference is given in the ratings to those accessories which can provide the full range of capability.

The set of ratings used in the Media Capabilities Matrix are as follows:

0   Not applicable, unsuitable

S   Generally suitable

a   Suitable when combined with *visual motion adapters*

b   Suitable when combined with *visual motion adapters* or projectable working *models*

c   Suitable only when used in conjunction with live instruction

d   Suitable when combined with *audio-visual integrators*

e   May contain certain three dimensional components such as real or oversize operating controls

f   Suitable when combined with *dissolvers*

g   Suitable when used in or combined with *visual random access devices*

X   Contains integrated response control of presentation

Y   Presentation can be controlled by separate response systems

MEDIA CAPABILITIES MATRIX

MEDIA CAPABILITIES MATRIX	PLANE (2D)	SOLID (3D)	LOCALITY (3D)	MOTION, FULL	MOTION, CYCLICAL	MOTION, LTD. EXCUR.	MOTION, CONCEPTUAL	COLOR	QUALITY	LOCALITY	SIZE/SHAPE/TEXTURE	TEMPERATURE	MOTION	KINESTHETIC CUES	SELECTION	SPECIFIC	CREATED	INDICATION	MANIPULATION	GROSS BODY MOVEMENT	INFORMATIVE	EVALUATIVE	CORRECTIVE	LINEAR	BRANCHING	ADAPTIVE	REPETITIVE
OVERHEAD TRANSPARENCIES	S	0	0	0	b	c	a	S	c	0	0	0	0	0	Z	N	N	Z	N	0	S	c	c	c	c	c	S
AUDIO TAPES	0	0	0	0	0	0	0	0	S	S*	0	0	0	0	Y*	N	N	U	N	0	S	S*	S*	c	S*	0	S*
2 X 2 SLIDES	S	0	0	0	a	c	f	S	d	0	0	0	0	0	Y*	N	N	Z	0	0	S	g	g*	c	g*	0	S
SOUND SLIDES	S	0	0	S	S*	S*	S	S	S	0	0	0	0	0	Y*	N	N	Z	0	0	S	g*	g*	c	g*	0	S*
FILMSTRIPS	S	0	0	0	S*	S*	f	S	d	0	0	0	0	0	Y*	N	N	Z	0	0	S	g	g	c	g*	0	S*
SOUND FILMSTRIPS	S	0	0	S*	S	S	S	S	S	0	0	0	0	0	Y*	N	N	Z	0	0	S	c	c	c	0	0	S*
MOTION PICTURES	S	0	0	S	S	S	S	S	d	0	0	0	0	0	N	N	N	Z	0	0	S	c	c	c	0	0	S*
SOUND MOTION PICTURES	S	0	0	S	S	S	S	S	S	0	0	0	0	0	N	N	N	Z	0	0	S	c	c	c	0	0	S*
MICROFORM	S	0	0	0	0	0	S	S	0	0	0	0	0	0	Y*	N	N	Z	0	0	S	g	g	c	g*	c	S
TEACHING MACHINES	S	0	0	S*	S*	S*	S*	S*	S	S*	0	0	0	0	X*	N	N	Z	0	0	S	S*	S*	S	S	0	S*
VIDEO RECORDING	S	0	0	S	S	S	S	S	S	0	0	0	0	0	X	N	N	N	0	0	S	c	c	c	D	0	0
LIVE TELEVISION	S	0	0	0	0	0	0	0	S	0	0	0	0	0	N	N	N	N	0	0	S	c	c	c	0	0	0
SLOW SCAN TV	S	0	0	0	0	0	0	0	S	0	0	0	0	0	N	N	N	N	0	0	S	c	c	c	0	0	0
PRINTED MATERIAL	S	0	0	0	a	0	0	0	0	0	0	0	0	0	N	N	X*	X*	0	0	S	c	c	c	c	0	S
PROGRAMMED TEXT	S	0	0	0	a	0	a*	S	0	0	0	0	0	0	X	X	X*	X	0	0	S	c	c	S	S	0	S*
PAPER SIMULATIONS	S	0	0	0	0	0	0	S	0	0	0	0	0	0	X	N	0	X	0	0	S	c	c	S	S	0	0
CHARTS	S	0	0	0	0	c	0	S	c	0	0	0	0	0	N	N	N	N	0	0	c	c	c	c	c	c	c
DISPLAY BOARDS	S	0	0	0	0	c	0	S	c	0	0	0	0	0	N	N	N	N	0	0	c	c	c	c	c	c	S
EC II	S	0	0	0	0	c	0	S	S	0	0	0	0	0	X	X	N	X	X	0	S	S	c	S	S	c	S
AUDI/POINTER	S	0	0	0	0	S	S	S	S	0	0	0	0	0	X	X	N	X	0	0	S	c	c	c	0	0	S
CPS 48	S	0	0	0	0	S	S	S	S	0	0	0	0	0	N	0	N	N	0	0	S	c	c	c	c	c	S
UNIVERSAL PROCESS TRAINER	S	0	0	0	0	0	0	S	c	0	0	0	S*	0	0	0	0	X	X	0	S	c	c	c	c	c	S
MODELS/MOCKUPS	S	S	S	S*	S*	c	0	S*	c	0	S	0	S*	0	0	0	0	Z	N	N	c	c	c	c	c	0	S
BACK LIGHTED PANELS	S	e	0	0	S*	S*	S*	S*	c	0	e	0	e	0	0	0	0	X	N	N	S*	S*	S*	S	S	0	S
ANIMATED PANELS	S	e	0	0	S*	S*	S*	S*	c	0	e	0	e	0	0	0	0	X	X	0	S*	S*	c	S	S	0	S
SIMULATORS	S	S	S	S*	S*	c	S*	S*	S*	S*	S	S*	S*	S*	0	0	0	X	X	X	S*	S*	c	S	S*	S*	S
REALIA	S	S	S	S*	S*	c	S*	S*	S*	S*	S	S*	S*	S*	0	0	0	X	X	X	S*	S*	c	S	S	c	S
COMPUTER ASSISTED INSTRUCTION	S	0	0	S*	S*	c	0	S*	c	0	0	0	0	0	X	X	0	X*	0	0	S	S	S	S	S	S	S

Figure 2

Media Capabilities Matrix

Z   Presentation not controlled by response

*   Rating applies only to some devices in this category

The X, Y, and Z ratings for response parameters reflect a bias on the authors' part. They are based on the belief that effective responses require independent participation of each student. Thus, a situation where one or more students in a class give an oral response resulting in a teacher changing a slide or overhead transparency is *not* considered to be a response-controlled presentation. The "Z" rating differs from a "0" in that respect. A "Z" rated medium permits the type of response indicated but does not have provision for direct control of the presentation other than by intervention of an instructor. An "0" rated medium, on the other hand, does not lend itself to control by the response at all.

The Media Capabilities Matrix and the Worksheet (Figure 1) provide a means for determining which generic media are suitable for a particular requirement profile. Wherever the Worksheet indicates a concern with a particular parameter, the column corresponding to that parameter is checked in the Matrix. The symbols in the Matrix provide indications of what generic media types are suitable and what constraints exist on that suitability. For example, an objective whose profile includes requirements for plane, full motion, and color visual; auditory quality; specific response; corrective feedback; and both linear and repetitive interaction would produce the following list of candidate media, with their associated constraints:

An Example

Sound-Filmstrip
- Needs live instructor for handling response, feedback, and linear interaction.
- Only some of these devices can provide full motion and repetitive interaction.

Motion Pictures
- Needs AV integrator for sound.
- Needs live instructor for handling response, feedback, and linear interaction.

Sound Motion Pictures
- Needs live instructor for handling response, feedback, and linear interaction.
- Only some of these devices can provide repetitive interaction.

Teaching Machines
- Needs live instructor to handle corrective feedback for a constructed response. (This is contrary to efficient use of these machines.)
- Only some of these devices can provide full motion, color, auditory quality, corrective feedback, and repetitive interaction.

15

Video Recording	• Needs live instructor for handling response, feedback, and corrective interaction.
	• Only some of these devices can provide repetitive interaction.
CPS-48	• Needs live instructor for handling feedback and corrective interaction.
Computer Assisted Instruction	• Only some of these devices can provide full motion, color, and auditory quality.

This list of candidates shows that only computer assisted instruction can handle this requirement in a fully automated fashion, while several options exist for media used in conjunction with live instruction. The choice among these options would depend on the requirements of other objectives and on the other factors discussed under "Usage" in the Foreword.

PART TWO
GENERIC MEDIA DESCRIPTIONS

3

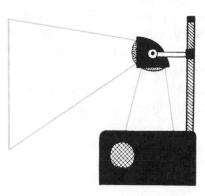

Overhead Transparencies

Overhead projection devices enable the projection of images transcribed on a clear acetate base as well as silhouettes of objects. The usual format is 8 inch x 10 inch transparencies; however 3 1/4 inch x 4 inch (lantern slides), 7 inch x 7 inch and 10 inch x 10 inch sized transparencies are sometimes used. In addition, certain overhead projectors may be adapted to show 2 inch x 2 inch slides. Conventional slide adaptation techniques involve a series of lenses and a single slide holder placed between the stage and the optical head. This method enables the slide image to be projected but precludes the full usage of overhead projection capabilities by preventing the projection of stage operations, i.e., pointing or writing. However, one dual-media overhead projector exists that enables simultaneous slide/transparency projection, and full usage of overhead projection capabilities with a 36 slide magazine.

Presentations involve manual positioning of the transparencies serially on the projector stage and proximity of the lecturer or an assistant to the projector (one unit has a motorized douser/transparency changer with a two-transparency capacity). Micro-switch dousing of the projector lamp each time a transparency is removed helps to reduce viewer eye fatigue. Operator eye strain can be reduced via a light shield accessory. The lens systems of overhead projectors are designed so that the projector can be placed in the front of a room, the availability of wide angle lenses enabling a very short projection distance. Overhead projection devices can be used in classrooms with normal ambient light. High intensity lamps are available on certain units where higher ambient light or long projection distances are anticipated.

Where projector locations are fixed, increased flexibility can be introduced by using a 360 degrees rotation swivel head machine which enables projection to different screen locations from a single source. To eliminate possible Keystoning effects, projection screens should be tilted slightly towards the audience. Projectors should be placed as low as possible to ensure that the body of the unit doesn't interfere with the line of vision of the audience.

Overhead transparencies can be easily prepared, either by drawing directly on transparent acetate or by using one of the many office duplicating machines that offer this capability. Unusual effects such as silhouettes and cut-outs are also easily prepared. Two superimposition methods are possible using overhead projectors. One involves stacking transparency layers on the stage; the other, projecting onto a writing surface (chalkboard, white-board, etc.) and adding details by writing on that surface. Because of their size, and accessibility during projection, overhead transparencies are easily masked to conceal information until it is needed.

Overhead projectors have the following advantages as an instructional medium:

- The speaker or instructor can operate the unit from the front of the room while facing the audience.
- The transparency placed face up on the machine top is completely legible to the speaker and may serve as his notes.
- The speaker can point to an item on the transparency and have this pointing appear silhouetted on the screen.
- Additional material can be written on and removed from the transparency during presentation.
- When equipped with a roll of transparent sheeting, the unit can serve as a projected blackboard. Material written on sheeting may be stored and a clean section rolled into position.
- By superimposing transparencies, models may be built or disassembled to better illustrate a point. In addition, working models can be silhouetted on the screen.
- Limited illusion of motion is also possible through use of special transparencies and polarizing spinner apparatus, or through Moire pattern producing gratings.
- Programs are easily modified by the deletion or insertion of transparencies.
- The time spent on each picture is completely under the instructor's control.
- The full range of photographic techniques (stop action, selective depth of field, air brushing, microphotography, etc.) is available.

The disadvantages of an overhead projector as an instructional medium are:

- The unit does not readily lend itself to rear projection since it requires proximity of lecturer and machine for most effective usage.
- Transparencies are large and present a storage problem.
- Location of previous segments of a presentation can be difficult and time consuming.
- Transparencies are easily marred or destroyed.
- Overhead projectors are large and cumbersome.
- A response and scoring capability is not inherent in or readily adaptable to the medium.

Overhead projection devices on the market are categorized in *data group 3* (corresponding to Chapter 3), and have been evaluated with respect to the following features:

- Physical Characteristics
    - Table Top Model
    - Floor Model
    - Carry Case
    - Weight Range
    - "Fold-away" Portable
    - 360 degrees Horizontal Swivel

- Illumination System
    - Incandescent Lamp
    - Tungsten or Quartz Halogen Lamp
    - Rated Lamp Life
    - High/Low Illumination Control
    - Spare Lamp Storage
    - Automatic Lamp Change
    - Semi-Automatic Lamp Change
    - "Spare Lamp in Use" Indicator
    - Lamp Ejector
    - Microswitch Douser
    - Stage Temperature

- Optical System
    - Condenser
    - Fresnel
    - Condenser and Fresnel
    - Glare Shield
    - Non-Glare Stage
    - Extra-Wide Angle Lens
    - Assorted Lenses Available
    - Built-in Lens Selection
    - Power Focus
    - Built-in Slide Projection
    - 2 inch x 2 inch Slide Adapter at Extra Cost
    - Simultaneous Slide/Transparency

- Writing Roll

4

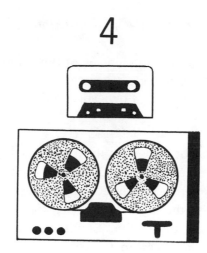

Audio Tapes

Audio tape recordings are a simple and economical medium for the storage and retrieval of sounds. They are widely used wherever the sound itself is an important part of the information being conveyed (music, language, etc.). Because of their convenience, they are also frequently used to convey verbal information either alone or in conjunction with some visual medium. Auditory presentation of verbal material is constrained by the strict linearity of the medium. Whereas with a printed text or most other visual media, the reader can set his own pace, and even re-read as desired, the audio media present material one word at a time at a predetermined rate. One can replay portions of recordings but with nowhere near the selectivity of re-reading.

Audio tape presentations have the following advantages as an instructional medium:

- Tapes provide alternate information channels for students with low reading skill levels.
- Tapes permit the rearrangement of sound materials through editing thus enabling the juxtaposition of material for comparison.
- Tape playback units can be small and portable.
- The auditory component or conditions of actual tasks may be preserved for future reference and analysis.
- Duplication of presentation is easy and economical.
- Student constructed response is possible with recorders for later analysis and interpretation.
- Exact timing of presentations is possible. Tape recorders run at pre-set speeds and the time to play a certain program may be computed in advance with accuracy.
- Limited branching capability exists on multi-track and random access machines.
- Tapes may be erased and reused.

The disadvantages of audio tapes as an instructional medium are:

- Lack of visual or tactile experiencing of the material.
- High susceptibility to outside distraction.
- Fixed rate of information flow—adjustment to learner's rate is generally impracticable.

Tape recording and playback devices incorporate a number of choices between sound quality and convenience. Tape speeds, for example, range from 1-7/8 inches per second to 7-1/2 inches per second in consumer machines, with higher speeds in studio equipment. Generally, the higher the speed, the better the sound quality but with attendant higher tape utilization. Similarly, the narrower the individual recording tracks, the more information that can be recorded on a given piece of tape; but the more susceptible it is to the effects of improperly aligned recording and playback heads.

Tapes themselves also involve these quality vs. convenience choices with the thinner tapes offering more tape (recording time) per reel or cassette but with more susceptibility to stretching, breaking, print-through,* etc.

Tape quality varies widely with respect to background noise, which can be particularly troublesome when the tape contains synchronization pulses for use with visual media. Low noise tapes may use a special coating (chromium dioxide) which requires different recording equipment than is used with regular tape. Another type of low noise tape uses the so-called calendered or burnished coating, which can be used with regular recorders and also has the advantage of promoting longer life of the equipment. Calendered tape is considerably more expensive.

Magnetic tape audio devices are categorized in *data group 4.* In addition to this data grouping, audio record and playback capabilities exist in certain audio-visual integrating systems (data group 18a) and on certain 16mm and 8mm projectors, sound filmstrips and slide projectors (data groups 7a, 7b, 6b, and 5).

Magnetic tape audio devices on the market have been evaluated with respect to the following features:

- Tape Loading
    - Reel to Reel
    - Cassette
    - Cartridge (a continuous loop magazine of audio tape)

- Audio Format
    - Monaural
        - Full Track
        - Half Track
        - Quarter Track
        - Multi Track (more than 4)
    - Stereo

*Print-through: A condition where the sound from one part of a tape can be faintly heard on another portion.

2 Track
4 Track
8 Track

- Operating Characteristics
    Recording Capability
    Playback Capability
    Separate Student Record Track
    Automatic Stop for Student Action
    Portable
    Tape Speeds (1-7/8, 3-3/4, 7-1/2, and 15 inches per second)
    Battery Powered
    117 VAC Powered
    Full Remote Control (enables control of all machine functions—i.e.,
        Play, Record, Fast forward, Reverse)
    Remote Pause Via Mike
    Remote Pause Via Foot Control
    Automatic Shutoff
    Automatic Tape Reversal
    Internal Speaker
    Requires External Speaker/Headset
    Random Accessing of Information
    Built-in Repeat for Review of Information

- Machine Output
    Speaker/Headset

- Machine Input
    Microphone (low signal level)
    Radio/Phonograph (high signal level)

5

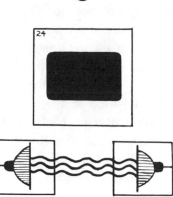

Slides and Sound Slides

A slide is a film transparency (35mm and less commonly "620," "120," "126" or "127" size film and also Polaroid camera film) usually mounted in a 2 inch x 2 inch cardboard, metal, or plastic frame. The inside frame dimensions (image area) vary according to the film size used, and may also be specially cut ("masked") to provide unusual image shapes. Single frame 35mm film (such as is used in filmstrips) and even 16mm film can also be mounted in 2 inch x 2 inch frames, although much of the potential image area is thereby wasted. Sometimes the film is mounted between two thin pieces of glass in order to protect the film and to prevent distortion due to film warping. (It should be noted that not all slide projectors can handle the increased thickness of glass mounts.) In addition to slides (2 inches x 2 inches), there are also oversized slides (2-1/4 inches x 2-1/4 inches), lantern slides (3-1/4 inches x 4 inches), and various mounted transparencies in standard sheet-film sizes (4 inches x 5 inches, 5 inches x 7 inches, etc.). The discussion that follows, however, is generally limited to the 2 x 2 formats.

Slide projection devices usually use some sort of magazine containing several slides. Magazine capacities vary widely. Some devices handle stacks of slides directly. Slides are handled in the projector mechanically, thus introducing potential equipment failures. This is generally outweighed, however, by the convenience of this medium. Control of the slide projector can be manual, or "automatic." Manual control can be either at the projector or through electrical remote control. This latter capability is especially convenient for rear projection and where the desired screen image size requires locating the projector some distance from the optimum instructor position. "Automatic" control has a variety of meanings in the sales literature. The most common automatic feature is the self timer which permits programmed slide changes at a fixed interval. This timer feature is more useful for display and home use than for instructional situations, however. Among the other more common "automatic" features are self-adjusting focusing and precise registration. The latter is important where visual "build-ups" are being used.

Projectors with remote-control capability can be used with a number of accessory devices including dissolvers (for cross-fading two or more projectors) and audio synchronizers or audio/visual integrators which tie the control of the projector(s) to magnetic tape sound tracks (see Chapter 18). Optical dissolvers are also available for some slide projectors as are tachistoscopic attachments for precise control of the exposure time of the projected image.

Sound-slide projectors integrate audio and visual presentations, with the slides controlled by pulses incorporated in or with the audio recording. A number of different pulse frequency codes are used so that some compatibility problems can occur with commercially available software. Many sound-slide projectors, however, have built-in pulsing/programming capability for local production of the audio portion of the presentation. Most sound-slide projectors use standard tape cassettes, although some tape cartridge and reel-to-reel types are also available. The principal problem with sound-slide presentations is loss of synchronization between sound and picture. Two machines overcome this problem by providing individual audio recordings packaged directly with each slide. A third machine which uses a standard tape cassette employs a pulsing technique which maintains synchronization during fast-forward and rewind of the tape.

Certain sound-slide projectors can also be programmed to stop the presentation in order to permit some student action such as practicing a skill, doing a workbook exercise or answering a question. Restart can be accomplished through a responder device (see Chapter 18) which requires the student to indicate the correct answer to a question before the sound-slide program continues.

Random-accessing of slides is a feature of some projectors. The use of this feature involves a quite different presentation approach from either regular instructor-run slide shows or programmed sound-slide presentations. Random-access projectors are treated separately in Chapter 18.

Slide projection devices have the following advantages as an instructional medium:

- The full range of photographic techniques (stop action, selected depth of field, air brushing, microphotography, etc.) is available.
- Tests may be incorporated into the medium.
- Slide sequence can be rearranged fairly easily to meet specific needs.
- Update of program is easily accomplished without extensive changes or expensive equipment.
- Slides can be easily made with any 35mm camera, enabling amateur productions.
- The time spent on each picture can be completely under the instructor's control.
- Small size of slides permits ease of storing.

The disadvantages of this medium are:

- Continuity of action is disrupted; only stop action demonstrations are possible.

Sound slide systems have all the above advantages with the exception that the slide sequence cannot be easily rearranged and the time spent on each picture is fixed.

Slide projection devices are categorized in *data group 5.* In addition to this data grouping, slide projection capabilities exist on certain overhead projection devices, random access systems, filmstrip, and sound filmstrip projectors (data groups 3, 18b, 6a, 6b, respectively). Certain teaching machines (data group 9) also use 2 inch x 2 inch slides.

Slide and sound-slide projection devices on the market have been evaluated with respect to the following features:

- Lens Type
  - Zoom Lens Available
  - Single Fixed Lens
  - Assorted Lenses Available

- Audio Characteristics
  - Sound-slide Device
  - Reel to Reel Audio Tape Loading
  - Cartridge Audio Tape Loading
  - Cassette Audio Tape Loading
  - Special Audio Synchronization Technique (slides stay synchronized when tape is run in "fast forward" or "reverse")

- Projection Technique
  - Front Projection
  - Built-in Rear Projection

- Illumination
  - Conventional Lamp
  - Hi-Intensity (designed for front projection in lighted rooms)

- Operating Characteristics
  - Automatic Timed Operation (slides advance automatically in a timed sequence)
  - Remote Control of Operations (varies from simple slide advance to both forward and reverse with remote focus)
  - Built-in Programming Capability (enabling the generation of tone cues for synchronization)
  - Built-in Audio Record Capability
  - Filmstrip Capability
  - Slide Previewer (enables operator to see each slide immediately prior to its being projected)
  - Portable
  - Cartridge Slide Loading (as opposed to circular or rectangular trays used for storage and loading)

- Machine Capacity
    - Up to 12 Slides
    - Up to 38 Slides
    - Up to 48 Slides
    - Up to 50 Slides
    - Up to 80 Slides
    - Up to 96 Slides
    - Up to 100 Slides
    - Up to 120 Slides
    - Up to 140 Slides

6

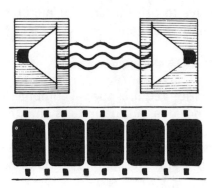

Filmstrips and Sound Filmstrips

Filmstrip projection devices enable the projection of a series of still pictures in color or black and white, using either front or rear projection techniques. Filmstrip devices are available to handle 35mm (single or double frame), 16mm and Super 8mm film. (Single frame 35mm format is similar to 35mm motion picture film, double frame 35mm format uses the same image area as 35mm slides.) The 16mm and Super 8 filmstrips are frequently loaded on reels or in cartridges. Continuous-loop filmstrips are handled by some machines.

Audio is incorporated into a filmstrip presentation by synchronization of record discs or magnetic tape with the filmstrip. Filmstrips can be advanced manually in response to an audible signal, or automatically in response to audible or inaudible signals. These accompanying signal and sound tracks are recorded independent of the processing of the film. Magnetic tape sound tracks can be easily erased and new information recorded, while modification of disc sound tracks requires complete re-recording of the programs with special equipment.

Filmstrip projectors have similar options to 2 inch x 2 inch slide projectors, such as various lenses, remote controls, and adapters for other projectable media. Remote controlled non-audio projectors can be used with some audio-visual integrators (sometimes requiring special adapters) to achieve sound-filmstrip capability.

Filmstrip projectors have the following advantages as an instructional medium:

- The sequence of pictures is fixed, ensuring that the material will be presented in the desired order.
- The time spent on each picture can be completely under the instructor's control.
- The filmstrip's small size allows for easy storage and handling.
- Filmstrip production equipment is portable, easy to operate, and usually inexpensive.
- The full range of photographic techniques (stop action, selected depth of

31

field, air brushing, microphotography, etc.) can be used.
- Some devices offer the possibility of animation, build-up, and motion sequences, dependent upon their pull down rate and registration.
- It is less expensive to print a series of pictures on a strip of film than to print, cut, and mount the same series in a set of slides.

The disadvantages of this medium are:

- Filmstrip production requires special equipment.
- The fixed sequence does not permit easy modification of the program.

Sound filmstrip systems additionally provide an alternate information channel for poor readers but then lose the capability to hold individual pictures as long as the instructor desires.

Filmstrip projection devices are categorized in *data groups 6a and 6b* (the latter being sound filmstrip devices). In addition, filmstrip projection capability exists on certain slide projectors (data group 5) and on single frame motion picture projectors (data groups 7a and 7b).

Filmstrip projection devices on the market have been evaluated with respect to the following features:

- Lens Type
    Zoom Lens Available
    Single Fixed Lens
    Assorted Lenses Available

- Projection Technique
    Front Projection
    Built-in Rear Projection

- Operating Characteristics
    Remote Control of Operations (varies from only forward to both forward and reverse operation with remote focus)
    Battery Operation
    Continuous Loop 35mm Filmstrip Capability
    2 inch x 2 inch Slide Capability
    Double-frame Filmstrip Capability
    Built-in Pointer

In addition to the above, sound filmstrip projectors have been evaluated with respect to the following features:

- Audio Characteristics
    Record Disc Speed
    Magnetic Tape Speed
    Recording Capability
    Built-in Speaker
    Remote Speaker
    Program Hold (restart dependent on student action)

7

Motion Pictures

A motion picture or "movie" is comprised of a series of still pictures in rapid succession producing an *illusion of movement*. There are three commercially available motion picture formats commonly used for educational purposes: 16mm, 8mm, and Super 8mm. The sixteen millimeter format is the most expensive but offers the highest scene illumination and the best resolution. Eight millimeter film format offers an inexpensive motion picture medium but is severely limited in resolution and picture brightness. Super 8 as a format is characterized by a film picture area 50 percent larger than 8mm film and offers higher scene illumination with better resolution capabilities, at moderate prices.

Sound films are projected at 24 frames per second, while silent films are projected at 18 frames per second. Audio capability is achieved with either a magnetic or an optical sound track on one edge of the film. An additional, more recent, method is to synchronize a separate cassette of magnetic tape with the film. Optical sound tracks are printed directly on the film stock when the film is processed. Changes in this audio part of the medium are not feasible except by reprocessing the entire film. Magnetic sound tracks are recorded after the processing of the film and can be easily erased and new sound recorded in its place, but the length of time for sound recording is physically constrained by the length of the film segment.

Both magnetic and optical sound track are physically displaced from the accompanying visual material so that the proper portion of the track is in contact with its sensing element for the particular visual frame being shown. Not all magnetic sound projectors have the same displacement, however. Efforts at standardization (with the sound 18 frames ahead of the picture) show progress but currently Super 8mm magnetic sound films and projectors are not always compatible.

Storage of film can be on open reels or in cartridges. Most cartridge projectors require no handling of the film. Minimizing handling of film is important both to simplicity of operation and preservation of the film itself. Self-threading capability also exists on many reel-to-reel machines although this is among the more poorly engineered features on many projectors.

Some projectors store film in continuous loops, either on an open reel or in a cartridge. Both self-threading and manual threading projectors for film loops are available. Continuous loops eliminate the necessity for rewinding film and also allow repetitive showing of materials.

Different motion picture projectors are used for 16mm, 8mm, and Super 8mm film. The so-called dual 8mm projector, however, can be used with either 8mm or Super 8mm film. Most silent 16mm projectors will damage optical soundtrack 16mm sound film. In general, sound projectors can handle silent film but *not* vice versa.

Control of forward, reverse, and stop action modes of operation is available remotely for some machines. However, the majority of devices have remote control of only forward operation. Stop action or single frame capabilities are available on most projectors. This is usually accomplished by mechanically stopping the film advance and shutter and interposing a heat filter, thus limiting the time a single frame may be shown and decreasing scene illumination. A further difficulty exists in alignment of the frame within the projector, causing focus shifts and frame separation to sometimes be visible, requiring subsequent realignment by the operator. A few more sophisticated devices are capable of projecting full brightness stills, but a focusing problem can still remain. Single frame capability becomes a further problem when sound motion systems are used. Continuing the audio while holding a single frame is only possible on devices which synchronize a separate magnetic sound track with the film. Qualitative judgment must be exercised regarding stop action capabilities in specific devices with relation to illumination, flicker, focus, and audio considerations.

Films have the following advantages as an instructional medium:

- Films provide alternate information channels for students with low reading skills.
- Films provide a continuity of action, showing action exactly as it occurs.
- Films provide "front seats" for many experiences. Demonstrations by experts can be performed, using all necessary equipment showing all essential steps, from just the right angle or aspect and at just the right speed for best analysis and learning.
- Films may be useful in testing. Because of the motion pictures' flexibility it may be stopped partially shown, or have tests inserted into the film.
- Time-lapse photography can enable the presentation of long term actions in moments. Conversely, slow motion and stop action capabilities permit analysis of intricate events.
- Films can provide a model for guided mental practice. Skills can be partially learned by watching a procedure on film and mentally performing the task without actual hands-on practice.

The disadvantages of this medium are:

- There is a lack of response and scoring capability.

- A controlled presentation environment is necessary. Darkness is required for most presentations, precluding note taking.
- Films run at an established rate and all viewers must receive information at that rate.
- Films are fairly expensive to produce. (Cost varies dependent upon film type, color vs. black and white, and if audio is included.)
- Updating films is relatively complex and expensive.

Motion picture projectors on the market are categorized in *data groups 7a and 7b,* which are 16mm and 8mm devices, respectively. In addition to these data groupings, motion visual capabilities exist in certain filmstrip machines, data groups 6a and 6b; certain teaching machines, data group 9; and video recorders and playback units, portable video recording systems, and TV projectors and monitors, data groups 10a, 10b, and 10c respectively.

Sixteen millimeter projectors have been evaluated with respect to the following features:

- Lens Type
    Zoom Lens Available
    Single Fixed Lens
    Assorted Lenses Available

- Audio Characteristics
    Optical Sound Track
    Magnetic Sound Track
    Recording Capability
    Built-In Speaker
    Remote Speaker
    Separate amplifier required (no speaker included)

- Projection Technique
    Front Projection
    Built-In Rear Projection

- Illumination
    Conventional Lamp
    Hi-Intensity Lamp (designed for front projection in lighted rooms)

- Operating Characteristics
    Automatic Threading Capability
    Remote Control of Operations (varies from forward only to forward
        and reverse as well as film speed and focus)
    Portable
    Silent Speed (18 fps) Capability
    Sound Speed (24 fps) Capability
    Slow Motion
    Single Frame/Still Picture Capability

Reel-to-Reel Loading
Continuous Loop Cartridge Loading
Selective Accessing (fast forward to selected location)

- Machine Capacity
  800 feet
  1000 feet
  1200 feet
  1600 feet
  2000 feet
  2200 feet
  2400 feet
  4000 feet
  5000 feet
  7000 feet

All 8mm projection devices utilize conventional illumination and are portable. They have been evaluated with respect to the following additional features:

- Lens Type
  Zoom Lens Available
  Single Fixed Lens
  Assorted Lenses Available

- Audio Characteristics
  Optical Sound Track
  Magnetic Sound Track
  Cassette Magnetic Tape Sound Track
  Recording Capability
  Built-In Speaker
  Remote Speaker

- Projection Technique
  Front Projection
  Built-In Rear Projection

- Operating Characteristics
  Automatic Threading Capability
  Remote Control of Operations
  Silent Speed Capability (18 fps)
  Sound Speed Capability (24 fps)
  Variable Speed Slow Motion
  8 fps Slow Motion
  6 fps Slow Motion
  54 fps Accelerated Projection Speed
  Still/Single Frame Capability
  Mixed Motion/Stop Capability (enables projection of motion and

single frame sequences in any combination under manual or automatic control)
Reel-to-Reel Loading
Cartridge Loading
Automatic Film Cartridge Changing
Continuous Loop Cartridge Loading

- Film Format
  Super 8mm
  Regular 8mm

- Machine Capacity
  50 feet
  100 feet
  200 feet
  300 feet
  400 feet
  600 feet
  800 feet
  1200 feet

8

Microform

A prime consideration in any library or learning resources facility is storage space. To minimize storage space, information may be photographed, optically reduced, and stored on film. The format of the optically reduced material is quite varied, existing in roll microfilm, microfiche or aperture cards. Roll microfilm can be either 35mm or 16mm stored in magazines, on reels or loose rolls. Microfiche can have either 98 images (NMA Standard) or 60 images (COSATI Standard) on a plate. Combinations of micro data and normal size data are termed aperture cards and are available in various sizes. In addition, computer outputs can be directly put on roll microfilm or microfiche (COM Fiche). The production, as well as update, of roll microfilm and microfiche requires specialized, highly complex equipment, but this medium does enable the storage and accessing of great numbers of pictorial or symbolic verbal information with a minimum of space.

Microform viewing devices use either rear projection or front projection techniques to "blow back" the reduced image to its original size. The majority of devices use only one method, but some devices are available that do both; and some also give paper copies if desired. Because of the small frame size, however, the amount of light available for front projection is limited, making microform generally unsuitable for group instruction. Determination of the desired magnification capability of a device depends on the original size of the information and the reduction rate used. The devices available have either a fixed or a variable magnification.

Of prime concern in the retrieval of data is the ability to locate it on a roll or fiche card. This is accomplished on roll microfilm with an elapsed footage counter or via bar coding. Footage counters are not accurate locating devices and the located film frame may require repositioning. Bar coding is another locating method in which a solid bar appears to move down the screen to an index mark, enabling high speed search for data, but this method will also require repositioning of film for single frame locating. An optimized locating technique which enables precise access of any frame of roll microfilm is available in a system which uses binary coding for each frame. Location of information on fiche cards is accomplished through manual X-Y positioning of the card with respect to the lens. A more effective locating technique involves stylus indexing, in which a pencil-like stylus is placed at a point on an index card causing the corresponding frame of fiche to be projected on the screen.

Microform has the following advantages as an instructional medium:

- Large amounts of information can be stored in a relatively small space, making this medium especially suited for detailed reference materials.
- Materials are of a convenient size for distribution and handling.
- Much reference documentation is commercially available at low cost.

The disadvantages of this medium are:

- The user is subjected to a number of factors which readily bring on fatigue, thus limiting the period of time when the medium is effective.
- A variety of formats are used so that different materials may require a number of devices.
- Special, complex, and expensive equipment is required to produce software.

Microform devices on the market are categorized in *data group 8* and have been evaluated with respect to the following features:

- Data Storage
    Microfilm
    Microfiche (a sheet or plate containing a number of separate minute images)
    Aperture Cards
    COM Fiche (computer output directly and put on fiche cards)
    16mm Roll Film
    35mm Roll Film
    35mm Film Strips
    Micro Jackets (clear carrier holders for loose strips or single film images)

- Projection Technique
    Front Projection
    Rear Screen Projection
    Fixed Size Screen
    Optional Screen Sizes
    Variable Magnification
    Fixed Magnification

- Operating Characteristics
    Battery Powered
    117 VAC Powered

Portable
Bar Code Indexing
Stylus Indexing
Counter Indexing
Manual Search Indexing
Magazine Loading
Cartridge Loading
Random Accessing of Information

9

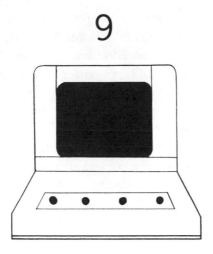

Teaching Machines

Teaching machines are devices which can present information, query learners, and have provisions for an overt response. They range in complexity from simple hand-held devices to complex digital computers used in computer assisted instruction (CAI). Teaching machines serve to mechanize linear, branched or adaptive programmed instruction. Linear and branched programs are discussed in Chapter 12. An adaptive program incorporates all the characteristics of a branched program in addition to having a more sophisticated decision-making process for remedial branching. Adaptive programs will branch the learner based on "history of performance" in addition to each individual response. Because of the complexity of branching based on "history of performance," computers or computer-like devices are used for mechanization of this type of programmed instruction.

Teaching machines present information via some audio, visual or audio/visual unit which is integral to, or controlled by, the device. Generally, teaching machines employ a "multiple choice" type of test. The user is required to indicate, by pressing a response button, a single-choice correct answer from a field of four or five possible answers. However, only a limited number of teaching machines employ branching type programs. In most cases pressing a "wrong answer" button only results in a "try again" direction to the learner (evaluative feedback). Two devices studied were compatible with a written constructed response. Most teaching machines do not, however, utilize constructed responses in linear programs.

When film is the visual medium, 16mm and 35mm formats are usually used for still displays with either 8mm or 16mm formats used for motion. Some devices use printed paper tape as the information carrier. In more sophisticated devices, such as multimedia carrels or CAI installations, television type displays are used.

Audio information is contained on either magnetic tape or pressed disc. In machines using a combination of audio and visual units there is need for the synchronization of media. This is accomplished, during normal modes of operation, by recorded inaudible tones or by electrical or mechanical linkage of media to response controls.

A typical sequence of events during man-machine interaction would be as follows: The teaching machine presents a "frame" of information to the user. This may be either an audio, visual or combination audio/visual presentation. The "frame" contains instructional subject matter information and directives for proceeding with the program. (For example, "when you have completed reading the text, answer the following questions by selecting the most correct answer from a choice of four.") The user then presses one of four buttons which correspond to the answer choices. If the selection is correct, the machine might advance the program to the next frame, or first expose the correct answer for student reinforcement and then advance the program to the next frame.

If the selection is incorrect the device could

a.   do nothing until the correct response is chosen and then proceed to next frame
b.   branch into a remedial loop
c.   present a "wrong answer" message, provide the user with additional information, and then instruct the user to make another selection.

The sequence of events is then repeated for the duration of the program.

Reinforcement, an indication by the teaching machine that the student has responded correctly, is a feature frequently included in machine design. This is accomplished by the illumination of a color coded lamp; the flashing of a "Correct Response" indicator; an audio tone or audio message; or a displayed printed message.

The recording of learner performance is accomplished by counting correct or incorrect responses utilizing electrical or mechanical counters or by a "punch card" device which may use cards that are computer compatible.

To expand the versatility of the teaching machine some manufacturers have included the capability to control external media. This is accomplished by external media switches or direct electrical link to response switches.

In the most common mode of operation all machines that were surveyed were student-paced. However, several machines had an optional testing mode where the device may control the time allowed to respond. An additional utilization for machine pacing is in drill type exercises.

Teaching machines have the following advantages as an instructional medium:

*   They combine the advantages of self-pacing without permitting the learner to skip over material.
*   They require overt responses from the learner.
*   Some teaching machines are useful in implementing branched pro-grammed instruction by removing the nuisance of constantly looking for page numbers.
*   Many machines have built-in scoring capability.

The disadvantages of this medium are:

*   Equipment complexity can introduce problems of both operation and maintenance.
*   Software is usually unique to a machine. The full range of commercial

programs are not available for any one machine.
- Custom production of software is often difficult and expensive.

Teaching machines on the market are categorized in *data group 9.* They may also be constructed by the combination of AV integrators (data group 18a), Responders (data group 18c), and suitable projection equipment.

Teaching machines have been evaluated with respect to the following features:

- General Features
    - Individual Student Unit
    - Hand Portable Configuration
    - Desk Top Configuration
    - Student Self Pacing
    - Reinforcement
    - Customized Program Required
    - Self Contained Programming Capability
    - Manufacturer's Format
    - Machine Pacing Option
    - Modularized System
    - Carrel Configuration
    - Computer Compatible
    - Random Access Information Retrieval

- Media and Media Control
    - Response Controlled Media
    - Manual Control of Media
    - Control of External Media
    - 16mm Film
    - Film Strip
    - 2 inch x 2 inch Slide
    - Magnetic Audio Tape
    - Audio Pressed Disc
    - Motion Visual
    - Still Visual
    - Audio
    - Cassette
    - Cartridge

- Response and Response Processing
    - Multiple Choice Response
    - Constructed Response
    - Response Counter
    - Permanent Record of Response

- Type of Program
    - Linear
    - Branched
    - Adaptive

10

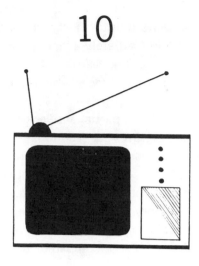

Television

Television is an electronic system of transmitting still and moving pictures with sound via transmission lines or through space. The system consists of equipment that converts light and sound into electrical energy and then reconverts that energy back into visible light and audible sound. Broadcasting is the most common type of transmission, where programs are radiated to viewers within the range of a given station. Closed circuit television (CCTV) is another type of system, and is frequently found in school and training centers. A CCTV system limits the distribution of its signal to only those receivers which are directly connected by transmission lines, or Microwave link. For purposes of this media selection system, television has been considered in three parts: *Live Television, Video Recording* and *Slow Scan Television.*

The principal uses of *live television* for instruction are: 1) telecommunication or the ability to observe an event at a distance from the event, and 2) magnification of the visual image. Quite often, the two uses are combined. Telecommunication is needed when the viewer must be separated from the event for any reason; i.e., audience capacity at the event, physical obstruction of the view, safety, logistics, etc. Telecommunication not only permits separation of a viewer from the event but also the dispersion of a number of viewers. Magnification through close-ups, microscopes, etc., is also a frequent usage of this medium. The more complex television techniques discussed below are rarely used in instructional live television because of the need for coordination of the efforts of many people in real time.

Video recording (most frequently, Video Tape Recording or VTR) is a vastly more flexible medium since it relieves time constraints on the "perfecting" of the instructional program and makes practicable a wide range of special effects. Not only can program material be edited and corrected, but multiple images can be superimposed, displayed simultaneously on a "split screen," and combined in an endless variety of ingenious ways. (Color television is especially flexible in providing a potential for visual image combinations.) Action can be shown at varying speeds, stopped or reversed. In addition to these program production advantages of video recording, there are also advantages due to short-term and long-term storage. Video recordings can be played back immediately (short-term storage) thus providing a medium for self-observation where the learning task requires practice of a skill. Long-term storage has the obvious advantages which make it comparable to motion pictures.

Slow Scan Television (SSTV) is a partial answer to the economics of television, where the number of individual pictures per second is "traded-off" against a number of technical equipment and transmission factors. The reader may be familiar with a somewhat slower than normal scan rate (10 pictures per second) from the widely viewed television transmissions of the earlier moon landings of Project Apollo. Even slower scan rates (1 picture every 10 to 40 seconds) were transmitted from interplanetary unmanned space probes and are currently being used in a few instructional situations. SSTV may be compared to filmstrips as far as image capability is concerned.*

Television has all the advantages listed earlier for motion pictures. In addition, it has the following unique advantages when used as an instructional medium:

- The familiarity of the average student with television minimizes distracting novelty effects of the equipment itself.
- The immediacy of live television adds dramatic impact and interest.
- The immediate playback capability of video recording permits effective analysis of live or on-the-spot action.

The disadvantages of this medium include the following:

- Live television imposes severe and sometimes unpredictable scheduling constraints.
- Equipment is considerably more complex than comparable motion picture devices.

Recorders and Playback Units

TV recorders may be purchased with either a color or monochrome-only recording capability. Some manufacturers offer conversion kits for adapting monochrome units to color.

Slow motion is the capability of a recorder to *play back* at a rate slower than the recording rate. It may be obtained with a fixed or with a variable speed control. Not all manufacturers offer both options in the same unit. Time lapse recording is the capability of a unit to *record* events at a rate slower than the playback rate. For example, one unit studied records at 7-1/2 inches per second for one hour of conventional mode operation, and records at 1-1/16 inches per second for 7 hours of time lapse operation. Accordingly, when events recorded in time lapse operation are played back in conventional mode the resulting effect is 7 hours of information viewed in one hour.

By obtaining a recorder with capability for variable motion time lapse

*For further discussion of SSTV see Bretz, Rudy. *A Taxonomy of Communication Media.* Educational Technology Publications, Englewood Cliffs, New Jersey, 1971, pages 106-108.

recording and stop action (freezing a single frame of action into a still picture for as long as desired), an instructor would be able to do a complete motion analysis or time sequence analysis of events for student learning.

Electronic editing is a desirable feature. Units having this capability contain electronic circuits, which, during the edit mode of operation, match incoming and previously-recorded video to eliminate "roll-over" and horizontal "break-up." This produces distortion-free editing and the smoothest possible tapes for professional appearance and reproduction. Editing capability may or may not conform to Federal Communications Commission Standards for broadcast equipment.

It is interesting to note that not all video players use magnetic video tape. One manufacturer uses 8.75mm film as the information carrying medium. The buyer should realize that, when purchasing this type of playback device, there are serious restrictions to be considered. No other manufacturer's tape or film can be played by the unit; all existing magnetic video tapes would have to be converted to the 8.75mm format, and editing for update requires the manufacture of a new film.

Video recorders and playback units on the market are categorized *in data group 10a* and have been evaluated with respect to the following features:

- General Capabilities
    Record and Play
    Record Only
    Play Only
    Monochrome
    Color
    Maximum Recording/Playing Time
    Suitcase Packaging

- Special Capabilities
    Color Adapter Available (at added cost)
    Slow Motion
    Variable Motion
    Stop Action
    Remote Control
    Electronic Editing
    FCC Standard Electronic Editing
    Audio V.U. Meter
    Play While Recording
    Time Lapse Recording
    Audio Dubbing

- Recording Format and Speed
    Manufacturers Format
    EIAJ Type 1 Format
    Recording Speed in Inches Per Second
    9.6
    8.57
    7.8

7.5
6.9
3.75
1.06

- Tape Size and Loading
  1 Inch Tape
  1/2 Inch Tape
  1/4 Inch Tape
  12-1/2 Inch Reel
  10-1/2 Inch Reel
  9-3/4 Inch Reel
  8-1/2 Inch Reel
  8 Inch Reel
  7 Inch Reel
  Cassette Loading

Portable Video Recording Systems

A portable video tape recording system comprises a video camera, battery pack, microphone, and a recording unit consisting of a tape transport and required operating electronics. Existing systems weigh from 20 to 33 pounds, including the battery pack. A monitor for immediate replay is included in some systems while others have no replay capability.

The combined features of self-contained power and light weight make this type of video recording system a dynamic and versatile training tool. However, not all of the portable systems' features are positive. Most systems record only monochrome. It should also be noted that a considerable amount of care must be exercised when handling and operating portable VTR equipment. The camera contains, in addition to a lens, a light-sensitive vidicon tube which is mechanically fragile. Rough handling or high intensity light inputs will damage the tube.

Battery operation time ranges from a low of 40 minutes to a high of 80 minutes before recharging is required. All manufacturers offer a battery charging unit as an optional accessory if the capability to "recharge" is not built into the recorder unit. The additional feature of system usage during battery charging time is included in most designs and implemented through the use of A.C. adapters. One system is unique in its power requirements; it is restricted to 117 Volts A.C. This feature severely impairs the freedom of being portable. Power considerations are, therefore, threefold:

- Battery operation, with the limitation of no use while batteries are charging
- Battery and 117 VAC operation, with the capability of use simultaneous with battery charge
- 117 VAC operation, with the limitation of the line cord operation.

Manufacturers have not as yet standardized the tape size, tape loading or recording format. Presently, most systems are designed for 1/2 inch tape. However, there are two systems (both made by the same company), which use 1/4 inch tape. The popular method of tape loading is on conventional 5 inch reel with most manufacturers looking into the development of cassette or cartridge systems. Recording formats vary from EIAJ Type 1 international standard to individual manufacturers' formats, which are unique to each system.

Portable video recording systems on the market are categorized in *data group 10b* and have been evaluated with respect to the following features:

- General Capabilities
  Playback
  Built-in Monitor
  Monochrome Recording
  Color Recording
  R.F. Output Signal
  Video Output Signal
  Record from TV Receiver
  Electronic Viewfinder
  Mechanical Viewfinder
  Optical Viewfinder

- Special Capabilities
  Stop Action
  Auto Search
  Sound Dubbing
  Video Editing
  Tape Footage Counter
  Video Signal Meter
  Audio Signal Meter
  Slow Motion
  Automatic Shut Off
  Elapsed Time Counter

- Recording Format and Speed
  EIAJ Type 1
  Manufacturer's Format
  7.5 inches per second
  7.9 inches per second
  11.25 inches per second

- Tape Size and Loading
  1/4 inch tape
  1/2 inch tape
  Reel to Reel
  Cassette

- Maximum Recording Time
  60 minute record
  40 minute record
  38 minute record

30 minute record
25 minute record
20 minute record

- System Weight
    Less than 35 pounds
    Less than 25 pounds
    Less than 20 pounds

- System Power
    117 VAC
    Battery
    Battery Usage 80 minutes
    Battery Usage 60 minutes
    Battery Usage 40 minutes

- Lenses
    Assorted Lens Capability ("C" mount lens)
    Zoom Lens Supplied
    Fixed Lens Supplied

Monitors and Projectors

Television monitors are best used for small group viewing. Monitors are built in two configurations, as CCTV units and as combination CCTV/Receivers. The CCTV models must be hardwired to a single source such as a TV camera or video player. The combination unit has the added features of receiving UHF and VHF transmissions. Available in various CRT sizes, the viewing areas range from 37 to 295 square inches. Both monochrome and color sets are built of solid state electronics, with one manufacturer offering a battery powered monochrome unit. To satisfy studio requirements, rack mounted single or multi-display units are available. Special features such as external horizontal and vertical synch inputs are included in some monitors for users requiring total external synchronization. Convenience features such as a standby circuit, instant turn-on (no waiting for warm-up), and an extension speaker jack are also offered.

The TV projector may be used for either front or rear screen projection in monochrome or color. Designed for large audience viewing, these units project images up to 15 x 20 feet under comfortable ambient light, with larger screen capabilities under theater lighting conditions. UHF and VHF tuners are integral to some units, while other projectors are dependent on accessories for broadcast signal conversion or are restricted to CCTV inputs.

The TV monitors and projectors on the market are categorized in *data group 10c* and have been evaluated with respect to the following features:

- General Capabilities
    Monitor
    Projector
    Color

Monochrome
Solid State
R.F. Reception
UHF Reception
VHF Reception
CCTV Input

- Special Capabilities
    Audio Input Jack
    Audio Output Jack
    Video Output Jack
    External Vertical Sync Input
    External Horizontal Sync Input
    Sync Output Jack
    Extension Speaker Jack
    Rack Mounted
    Multi-Display
    Stand-By Circuit

- Power Requirements
    117 VAC 60 Hz
    220 VAC 50 Hz
    Battery Power

- CRT Size and Viewing Area
    CRT in Inches
    5
    9
    10
    12
    16
    19
    23
    25

    Viewing Area in Square Inches
    37
    44
    71
    88
    125
    172
    270
    282
    295

Telestrator

The Telestrator introduces another element of flexibility into televised presentations, allowing instructional material to be adapted in accordance with the audience requirements. It puts the presentation techniques of overhead transparency projectors at the disposal of an instructor using live TV or video recording.

This device enables the operator to print, draw, diagram, pictorialize, analyze, and annotate right into any televised picture. The composite picture produced is viewed immediately by both the operator and the audience, as it is written. Using a stylus, the instructor writes on a hard transparent position-sensitive surface which lies over the televised image on his monitor. By selection of switches on the control panel, solid lines, dashes, dotted lines, and circles in several choices of width are possible. The written graphics are available in shades of black and white, colors or even in plaid or polka dot patterns, and may be stored and recorded on simple audio type cartridges and recalled to appear on the screen at any time, on command and in registry over any background visual. When combining the device with a second TV camera, a live picture can be brushed into any scene with the stylus. This insert can be a cameo shot of an individual or a point of interest. The new visual can also be painted over the entire picture.

The Telestrator is a product of:

Telestrator Industries, Inc.
166 East Superior Street
Chicago, Illinois 60611

Responsive Television

Selection Response control of television presentation (both auditory and visual) is possible using a proprietary system known as Responsive TV. This system uses standard "special effects" (vertical, horizontal or quadrant split screen) to provide alternative materials in a *branching* strategy. A responder unit, inserted between any video playback unit and monitor, provides selective blanking of the screen. In effect, the student sees on a *portion* of the TV screen and hears, on a headset, an appropriate presentation as a result of his pressing one of four response push-buttons. Digital data outputs are also provided for recording of student responses.

Responsive TV is a product of:

Data-Plex Systems, Inc.
164 Mason Street
Greenwich, Connecticut 06830

TV Production Equipment

The equipment described in this chapter is concerned with the *user* of instructional television rather than the producer of TV programs. Experience shows, however, that the amateur TV production virus is highly contagious, especially when one already has invested heavily in playback equipment. The immediate replay capability permits seeing and correcting mistakes so that with some patience anyone can produce programs of quality that at least satisfy themselves.

11

Printed Materials

As used in this book's media selection system, the term *printed materials* refers to all textbooks, workbooks, pamphlets, and single-copy sheets with the exception of *programmed instruction texts* and *paper simulations,* which are treated separately in Chapters 12 and 13, respectively. The information in *printed materials* may be contained in words, drawings or photographs.

Printed materials have the following advantages as an instructional medium:

- Each person can proceed at a rate determined by his particular abilities and interests.
- Materials may be scanned and essential points extracted without having to sit through an entire presentation.
- Different aspects and viewpoints may be studied at the same time, and repeated, restudied, or referenced by the student as often as necessary.
- Learning may be accomplished at any convenient time or place.
- Materials may be outlined or underlined by the student, highlighting points and areas of interest. This provides student involvement as well as aiding later reference and review.
- No elaborate or expensive equipment is needed to convey the information.
- Visuals (i.e., photographs, diagrams, overlays) may be incorporated with text, illustrating concepts or points and increasing interest.
- High-volume printing of materials can result in much lower costs than the production of audio-visuals.
- Supplementary materials may be written and incorporated into textbooks. New pamphlets or fly sheets may be generated.
- Texts or a lecture series may be accompanied by workbooks which are keyed to facilitate learning by requiring the student to recall and integrate the information previously presented.
- When printed materials are used in conjunction with an instructor, they

enable a standardization of information. Each student is exposed to the same basic information which then can be explained and added to by the instructor. In addition, this material supplements the knowledge of the instructor.

- Local production and reproduction of materials is fast and inexpensive with generally available equipment.

The disadvantages of printed materials are:

- They rely heavily on the reading ability of students.
- They are a one-way medium. A student cannot ask for immediate clarification in most uses of this medium.

Printed materials are not associated with any particular instructional hardware. Hence there is no printed material data group.

12

Programmed Instruction Texts

Programmed instruction is a system of learning in which the subject matter is systematically organized into logical sequence and then broken down into small, discrete steps, each one building on the preceding step. A learner can progress through the sequence at his own rate and is reinforced by being given an evaluation of his response immediately after making it.

There are two chief types of programming. The first and most frequently used is the linear format. This type requires the learner to construct his own response to all questions in the program. The linear program has a single learning path. All students taking a linear program will receive the same information. There are no branches or detours which allow faster progress for the more capable student, nor does it provide more help for the less capable student. Linear programs are based on a learning model which emphasizes a schedule of rewards for "correct behavior."

The second type of programming is the branched type (sometimes called Intrinsic Programming). In the branched program, the learner is presented a single coherent idea or piece of information and then is tested by multiple choice questions. If he understands, he proceeds on to the next idea. If his response is incorrect, he is given new material designed to correct his deficiency. Each segment of remedial material is specifically designed to correct the misunderstanding he has exhibited by his choice of response. He is then queried again. If he now understands the original idea, he goes on to new information. If he still does not understand, he is instructed again. Branched programs are based on a learning model which emphasizes the two-way communication of a tutorial situation.

Variations exist on these two basic types, such as the use of multiple choice type questions in otherwise linear format and "fast track" branches through linear programs (sometimes called "forward gating"). Linear and branched programs as well as their variations can be presented effectively in a textbook format.

Programmed instruction texts have the following advantages as an instructional medium:

- Each person can proceed at a rate in accordance with his particular abilities and interests.
- Learning may be accomplished at any convenient time and place and can be repeated or restudied as desired.
- As a result of the program development process, materials are organized and sequenced in a proven, advantageous manner for learning.
- The difficulty and conceptual level of the material may be adapted to varying student populations. Both content and writing style can be simplified in branches designed for poor readers or for students with low intelligence levels.
- Cost per student is quite low, if used for stable subjects in high volume.
- In linear programming the student is given the correct response and reinforced immediately after each response.

The disadvantages of programmed texts include the following:

- It takes longer to write material in programmed instruction format and perform the validation trials, thus raising the initial cost compared to other printed materials.
- It is difficult to use a programmed instruction text for reference. The format does not lend itself to easy accessing of information.
- Branched texts are awkward to use because of constant searching for different pages.
- Linear texts are frustrating for students who are forced to go through sequences covering material they already know.
- The organization of material can discourage independent inquiry and creative thought.
- Programmed instruction texts rely heavily on the reading ability of the student.

In addition to text format, programmed instruction techniques are used with teaching machines (Chapter 9), computer assisted instruction (Chapter 17), and various projector and response system combinations.

Since there is no P.I. text hardware, no data group for this medium is included.

13

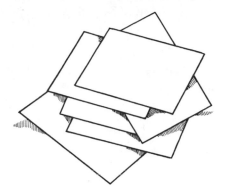

Paper Simulations

Certain subject matters are effectively approached by a strategy in which the learner must request each piece of information which he receives. This strategy is used in some management games and as a motivating approach in lower primary grades. It is also the effective strategy of practical trouble-shooting exercises.

In trouble-shooting, the individual learner has the opportunity to develop his own approach to a problem. In most other applications, however, a teacher or resource person is the information source for a whole class. The paper simulation is a means whereby this strategy can be individualized. It consists of a number of pieces of information which are hidden from the student. This can be test values on a schematic diagram, identifications or facts about components or areas on a pictorial viewer, or written answers to questions. This information is concealed by opaque tape or other substance which must be removed in order to reveal the information. It thus provides a record of what information was requested so that the learner's approach to the problem can be evaluated. In some simulations, the learner is instructed to sequentially number his inquiries as he makes them.

Paper simulations share with branched programmed instruction the problem of requiring the producer to anticipate many alternate learner actions and of providing "true" but irrelevant information. They share with other printed materials the economy of reproduction and ease of portability. They have been proven as effective training vehicles in trouble-shooting exercises where costs, logistics, and safety are overriding considerations.

Paper simulations have the following advantages as an instructional medium:

- They place a greater requirement on the learner to "think through" a problem.
- They share with other printed materials the ability to be used at any convenient time and place.
- In technical training, they permit analyses of situations which would otherwise be unsafe to personnel or equipment.

The disadvantages of this medium include the following:

- They only deal in static visual cues or in cues which can be verbalized.
- They require more abstract thinking than may be required by the task being taught.

Paper simulations do not require specific instructional hardware and so are not included among the data groups.

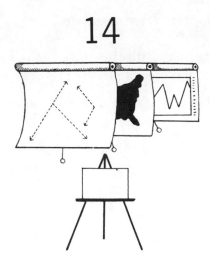

14

Wall Charts and Display Boards

Wall charts are prepared diagrams or pictorials on paper, cloth or plastic sheets for classroom use. The availability of photographic emulsions which can be put on any of these bases makes chart production from smaller artwork feasible and also permits small paper copies of the chart for student note-taking. Charts made from translucent plastic may be printed on the reverse side so that the front can be drawn upon with grease-pencil or water soluble ink during the presentation and then wiped clean again. Charts are generally less bother while being used than projected visuals (though more trouble to store and set up) and can be made in any ratio of height to width.

Display boards are any two dimensional medium for the display of non-projected visuals. This includes large writing surfaces such as chalk-boards and white-boards (the latter using erasable ink markers which are dust-free) and a variety of boards to which things can be attached. Some of the latter are:

- Magnetic Boards—boards to which magnets adhere. Paper may be held against the board by light weight, inexpensive magnets. Magnets may also be obtained cut in various shapes such as letters, symbols, lines, etc.
- Felt boards—special plastic backing adheres to the felt but can be readily removed and reused. A variety of letters, symbols, etc. is available with this backing.
- Cork boards—boards to which objects can be attached by pins or thumbtacks.

Many chalk and white boards also serve as magnetic boards.

Wall charts and display boards have the following advantages as instructional media:

- They require fewer environmental adjustments than projected visuals.
- Display boards enable an instructor to "build-up" the materials at a rate and manner compatible with student learning.

Among the disadvantages of these media are:

- They rely heavily on the effectiveness of a live teacher.
- Storage of charts and pre-cut pieces can present problems.

Because wall charts and display boards are so frequently custom made, no data group has been prepared for these media.

15

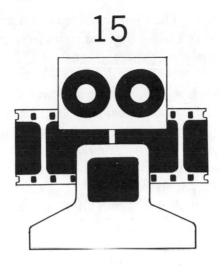

Special Devices

Some commercially available devices do not fit into the generic media classification scheme used in this book's media selection system, either because they use unique software or because standard software is used in a unique way. Four of these devices are included in the Media Capabilities Matrix and are described below.

ECII Programmable Simulator

The ECII is a training device which is designed primarily for teaching the proper trouble-shooting technique required in the testing and repair of a system or piece of equipment. The following programmable components are incorporated in this device:

- Pictorial/schematic display overlay—This assembly is mounted on the ECII directly in front of the student and provides a pictorial and/or schematic representation of the system to be taught. It contains up to 96 surface messages, switches, and indicator lamps, and provides the means by which the student performs simulated tests and component replacements.
- 35mm slides—These slides provide instructions, questions, waveforms, machine part pictures, or diagrams to the student. Each program can accommodate up to 100 slides.
- Magnetic tape cassette—Control signals are programmed into the ECII by this unit for the malfunctions, tests, or replacements which are to be simulated. Control of the 35mm slides is also a function of the taped program.
- Meter scale—When applicable, this scale provides simulated instrument readings to the student.

By pushing a button the system is "bugged" with one or more of 25 programmed malfunctions. The student interacts individually with the device to perform the simulated tests and component replacements required to locate and correct the malfunction. As a function of student responses and the control programming of the magnetic tape cassette, visual displays are provided as instant feedback to the student showing him the simulated result of his actions. A timer and two counters on the instructor's panel are used to measure student proficiency.

The major advantages of the ECII are:

- Actual equipment is not required for training.
- Minimal instructor services required. There is no need to bug or debug equipment, nor is an instructor required while the student is proceeding with the exercise.
- The student receives immediate feedback concerning his actions.
- Student proficiency is measured.
- This device's application is not limited to one particular piece of equipment or system.

The ECII is manufactured by:

Educational Computer Corporation
1540 Lancaster Avenue
Paoli, Pennsylvania 19301

Audi-Pointer

The Audi-Pointer is a portable audio-visual, console device which provides a means of presenting recorded lectures with associated visuals to small groups of students. It incorporates a viewing screen which can accommodate printed graphic materials up to 11 inches x 17 inches and a taped program controlled light which automatically high-lights the exact point of the drawing under discussion.

The pointer light appears in the drawing as a 1/8 inch illuminated disc. It can be controlled to blink or move back and forth to underscore and trace circuits or outlines. One channel of a standard stereo cassette provides the pointer control signals. The other channel contains the lecture narrative. Headphones permit complete privacy for the student if desired.

Student interaction with the device is accomplished by an "answer pen." At appropriate times during the lecture, the student is asked a question based on the previous discussion. He answers by placing the answer pen at the proper point on the viewing screen. The tape program is automatically paused and will not resume operation until a correct answer is registered or an overriding control is operated.

The major advantages of the Audi-Pointer Learning System are:

- Self paced learning—Controls enable the student to pause, rewind, go backward or forward as required.
- Standard graphic materials are used—The console can accommodate engineering drawings, blueprints, schematics, photographs, and printed half tones. Students can make notes on these graphics and retain for future reference.
- Easily programmable—One model of the Audi-Pointer incorporates all the necessary components required for producing and showing the narration and the pointer light programs. (Playback only models are available at reduced cost.)
- Minimal instructor time is required—Simple operating controls permit students to operate the device without instructor assistance.

The Audi-Pointer is a product of:
      Visual Educom, Inc.
      4333 S. Ohio Street
      Michigan City, Indiana 46360

**Mobile Training and
Briefing Console (CPS-48)**

This device is a self-contained, mobile, multi-media rear projection unit. It warrants special attention because of a patented optical system which focuses projected 2 inch x 2 inch or lantern slides on the light table or stage used for overhead transparencies. This makes the full range of overhead techniques (superimpositions, write-ons, pointing, etc.) available to the instructor using slides as the basic medium. The device also includes provisions for sound or silent motion pictures (not projected through the transparency stage), a second 2 inch x 2 inch slide or filmstrip projector and a tape recorder. These units are mounted inside the console and are remote controlled by a hand-held unit.

The physical dimensions of this unit are 91 inches high by 74 inches long by 31-1/2 inches deep when the built-in 36 inches x 48 inches screen is used. It weighs approximately 600 pounds. The user can specify the motion and slide projectors as well as the tape recording system desired.

The CPS-48 is a product of:
      Hoppmann Corporation
      5410 Port Royal Road
      Springfield, Virginia 22150

Universal Process Trainer (UPT)

The Carmody UPT is a training device which can be used to simulate the flow and control of various complex processes (i.e., petroleum refinement, chemical synthesis, food processing, etc.). It is suitable for use during initial familiarization training of inexperienced trainees as well as follow-up proficiency training of experienced process control personnel. It consists of a display board, a program board, and a control console.

The top portion of the display board is used to graphically portray the process by means of magnetically attached symbols and flow lines. During initial training sessions of new operators, knowledge of equipment locations, equipment relationships, and flow of the process can be readily taught. As training progresses to actual operating exercises and problems, the graphical display of the process provides a convenient visual reference of process configuration and flow to assist trainee decision making. The lower portion of the display board provides the simulated instrumentation and controls of the process (as would be found in the "control room"). A standard complement of 24 interchangeable instrument modules and a fixed multi-point indicator are used. Controlled manually from the control console or automatically by the program board, the instruments can depict normal readings and relationships as well as readings that are indicative of a malfunction or emergency. The instrument modules also contain the operating controls of the process. Trainees learn through actual performance as they set up the controls and monitor the instruments. They also learn trouble-shooting techniques through simulated problem analysis as the training exercises progress from normal operations to malfunction or emergency problems.

Automatic control of instrument readings to signify normal operations, malfunctions, or emergencies is accomplished through the patch board wiring of the program board.

Through various switches and potentiometers on the control console, the instructor can control the instrument modules of the display board and set up normal or emergency process conditions. By observing trainee's reaction and response time, the instructor can regulate the training for maximum effectiveness.

The main advantages of the Carmody Universal Process Trainer are:

- Programming flexibility—All major parts of the trainer can be easily set up to depict any process.
- Active student participation—Students are required to manipulate controls, monitor instruments, and perform problem analysis as would be required in the process control room.

The Universal Process Trainer is a product of:

Carmody Corporation
2361 Wehrle Drive
Buffalo, New York 14221

Each of these special devices is unique. Therefore, no comparative data group can be produced.

16

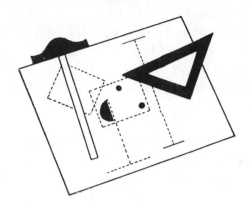

Custom Learning Aids

Custom learning aids are used where the subject matter is too complex for verbal, symbolic, or simple pictorial presentation; when three dimensionality is essential; or when principles and relationships can best be illustrated by physical objects and real actions. The custom learning aids category includes realia, simulators, models and mock-ups, animated panels, and back-lighted panels.

Models and Mock-Ups

Models and mock-ups are three dimensional representations of objects which differ from the real object in size, material, and/or functional capability. They may be constructed in a manner which permits easy disassembly or may be made of transparent material so that the learner may see internal functional relationships. Strictly speaking, a mock-up is full size while a model is an over- or under-size scale representation. However, the terms are frequently used as if they were interchangeable.

Models are most frequently used to illustrate both static and dynamic spatial relationships. However, they can also be used for physical analogies.

Animated Panels

Animated panels are essentially two dimensional display devices for illustrating mechanical actions. Individual parts are often color-coded to aid in differentiation. Motion can be derived from electromechanical devices (motors, solenoids, etc.) but more frequently is provided manually. This latter approach is not only more economical but also permits the motion to be slowed down or stopped to illustrate critical relationships.

Backlighted Panels

Backlighted panels are illuminated display boards which present functional diagrams in a number of conditions or states. There are two basic types of backlighted panels, one of which shows all elements of the diagram but uses lights in the diagram to accent the particular parts requiring immediate attention. The second type uses a dark screen (like a rear-projection screen) on which only the illuminated portion of the diagram is visible.

A frequent use of backlighted panels is to illustrate the functional relationships within an equipment system resulting from the operation of various controls. Such panels include a set of controls and electronic or electromechanical logic circuits to tie the controls to the diagram illumination.

Simulators

The term "simulation" carries a variety of meanings in the education and training field. Various games, both computer-based and self-contained, are used to simulate situations (see *Paper Simulations,* Chapter 13 and *Computer Assisted Instruction,* Chapter 17). Generally speaking, however, a *simulator* is a functional physical simulation, usually of an equipment system but also occasionally of an environment.

Equipment simulators are used to train personnel in such tasks as operation, emergency procedures, trouble-shooting, and maintenance of the simulated system. They may cost anywhere from a fraction to several times the cost of the equipment they simulate. They offer several advantages over realia. They can be designed to provide greater control over learning by incorporating instructor monitoring of learner actions and cues, situational freezes and/or recording so that specific behavior can be critiqued in depth. They are also designed so that personnel and equipment can be protected from the consequences of erroneous behavior.

Simulators may also be designed so that complex skills can be learned incrementally. Component tasks can be learned individually and then integrated.

Realia

Realia is any actual object used in learning about the object. Two broad classes of realia are *in-context* and *out-of-context* objects.

In-context realia is the basic medium of on-the-job training (O.J.T.) and field trips. It presents substantial logistics problems and can interfere with other on-going activities. In some cases it can also present hazards to personnel and equipment. For these reasons, the use of in-context realia requires careful planning and control. Its principal advantages are high "transfer of learning" and motivation.

Out-of-context realia generally offers more favorable circumstances for control and more flexibility in planning and utilization.

Realia, generally, does not provide much self-instructional capability. Most applications require the services of a teacher and/or resource person. Occasionally it can be combined effectively with other self-instructional media.

17

Computer Assisted Instruction

The computer performs two major functions in education. These are administration and individualized instruction. In addition, computers are sometimes used for research and counseling. The great advantage of the computer is that it possesses both memory and logic.

As an instructional medium, the computer can be programmed to:

- Present instructional material
- Question for understanding
- Remember all responses
- Classify responses
- Analyze responses
- Adapt an instructional sequence based on the cumulative trend of a student's responses

Computerized instruction can take many forms. In its most basic configuration, the learner usually interacts with the computer via a keyboard console similar to a typewriter, and a cathode ray tube (CRT) for display of information. The computer presents verbal material on the CRT or typewriter and records the responses the student makes on the typewriter. Student performance scoring is accomplished automatically with the computer storing the data.

As CAI configurations grow in complexity and usefulness a more diverse array of input-output devices are utilized. In addition to the popular keyboard console the learner may have a "light pen" to use as a response (input) device. The student can react to a picture on the cathode ray tube by placing the light pen at specific locations on the viewing surface and this action will be sensed by the computer and evaluated. Some types of information presentation (output) devices are:

- Rear screen motion picture projectors
- Rear screen 2 inch x 2 inch slide projectors
- Video tape players
- Random access motion and still film projectors

- Microfilm projectors
- Tape recorders for audio information, both random access and conventional

In these more complex configurations, the computer essentially *manages* the use of other media such as are described in the earlier chapters of this book.

The input-output device combination is called a *terminal.* One computer is capable of operating many terminals, each one virtually independent of the others. The terminals can be located several miles from the computer and from each other. Some terminals can be connected to the computer via conventional telephone circuits offering the possibility for individualized instructional services in the home.

The *principal advantage of CAI* is its ability to approximate human instructional capabilities (including adaptive strategies) while retaining the standardization, objectivity, and reliability of programmed instruction. However, this view of CAI as an idealized teacher can be overdone. While the computer does not get tired, or impatient, and does not forget, it *can* get sick, be stubborn, lack understanding, and even has been known to babble incoherently.

CAI can also provide automatic collection and processing of data concerning both learner performance and course material effectiveness.

Among the disadvantages of CAI are the following:

- The initial equipment investment is high.
- Equipment complexity results in a continuing requirement for skilled maintenance personnel.
- Development of programs requires additional skills (computer languages) beyond subject matter expertise and instructional capability.

CAI installations are custom designed and may include a number of computer controlled media devices. The various data groups for slide projectors, motion picture projectors, etc., can be quite useful in designing a CAI system but no data group can be produced for CAI per se.

18

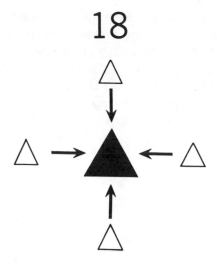

Accessory Devices

Various types of equipment are available which allow the effective conversion of one medium into another or provide expanded capabilities for a medium. These include *visual motion adapters, audio-visual integrators, visual random access devices,* and *responders.*

Visual Motion Adapters

Two techniques exist which can add cyclical* and conceptual* motion to otherwise still visual presentation. Both are patented processes. Technamation is used with overhead projectors and 2 inch x 2 inch slides. Visionetics is used with overhead projectors, printed materials, and programmed text.

Technamation is a custom technique. Although a kit is available for amateur production of simulated motion transparencies, sophisticated devices are required to produce high quality training slides or transparencies. The Technamation process starts with conventional 35mm slides or transparencies which are photographs of artwork or original subjects. Custom artwork is then prepared for the portions of the image that are to "move" and then, special materials are added to the basic slide or transparency. These materials polarize the projected light in one or more planes. When projected in normal fashion, the screen image is unchanged from the original. When a motion adapter is added to the projector, a rotating disk of polarized material alternately stops and transmits the polarized light coming through the "motion" parts of the slide or transparency thus producing the illusion of movement.

The cost of Technamating customer supplied artwork is fairly expensive for the first slide with succeeding copy slides running much cheaper. Overhead transparencies can be Technamated in small quantities for approximately half of the first slide cost. Motion adapters are available to fit all slide projectors and overhead projectors. Some models include variable speed and direction control.

*These terms are defined in Chapter 1.

Visionetics is also a custom technique. Artwork for both printing and transparency production is altered by dividing the image into fine, parallel lines having little noticeable effect by themselves. Movement of a special transparent grid over this artwork causes so called Moire patterns to shift in predictable fashion giving a motion illusion. When the process is used in texts the user manually moves the grid across the illustration to see motion. A motor-driven actuator grid is available for use of this technique on overhead transparencies. The stage containing the actuator grid can be affixed to any standard overhead projector. Normal transparencies may be projected without any interference.

Audio-Visual Integrators

Audio-visual integrators, often called *synchronizers,* are used to integrate an audio tape presentation with a silent visual medium such as 2 inch x 2 inch slides, filmstrips, and less frequently motion pictures. This is usually accomplished by recording inaudible pulses on the tape which are used to trigger remote control functions of the projector. Other techniques include pencil marks and metal foil strips on the tape.

The script audio may be incorporated on the same tape with the signaling pulses, or the control tape may run other tape recorders containing the script audio. Devices may be advanced, turned on and off, or shifted into an automatic stop response mode, stopping on coded signals and not advancing until manually directed to do so. Integrators with this feature will also accept *responders* and can be used in automated teaching programs.

Production of the control tapes for the audio-visual integrators may be accomplished by first recording the script and then entering code pulses while listening to the playback. Most devices incorporate program recording and pulse coding in one unit. A few devices require separate tone generating and programming devices, which can be bulky, complicated, and expensive. Integrating devices are also available that will integrate any tape recorder into the controlling system enabling the use of in-inventory equipment and a cost savings.

Reasonably priced devices exist to integrate as many as three machines at once or to control three operations of a single machine. Reverse synchronization enabling back tracking during a presentation is not usually possible; all systems reviewed except one are thrown out of synchronization by reverse operation and require restarting from the beginning.

Audio-visual integrators are categorized in *data group 18a.* In addition to this data grouping, audio-visual integration is accomplished by certain sound filmstrip machines, sound slide machines, 8mm motion picture devices, and teaching machine systems—data groups 6b, 5, 7b, and 9, respectively.

Audio-visual integrators on the market have been evaluated with respect to the following features:

- Audio/Control Tape Characteristics
    Reel to Reel Loading
    Cassette Loading
    Continuous Loop Cartridge
    Separate Reel to Reel Tape Recorder Required
    Separate Tape Recorder Required

- Control Method
    - Signal Pulse
    - Pencil Mark

- Operating Characteristics
    - Built-in Programming Capability (enabling the generation of tone cues for synchronization)
    - Special Programming Device Required
    - Built-in Audio Record Capability
    - Remote Control Feature (usually limited to stop/start)
    - Automatic Stop Feature
    - Reverse Synchronization Capability
    - Number of Machines or Operations Controllable
    - Capability of Accepting Signal Pulse from Either Audio Track

Visual Random Access Devices

During the course of learning it often becomes necessary to refer to information already presented. This situation can exist both for a lecturer as well as an individual student viewing a training program. To back-track through every slide or through a whole roll of film, or to start completely over from the beginning is time consuming and tends to reduce attention and motivation. Similarly, it may be desired to skip ahead or otherwise branch to a new area of the material. Through random access equipment, the desired portion of a program may be selected without viewing intervening frames. Random access systems are composed of slide projectors, movie projectors or filmstrip projectors in combination with digital servo units for the addressing and accessing of projection frames. Accessing of information requires the manual positioning of remote dials, thumbwheels, or pushbuttons to the appropriate frame number. The capability exists in random access systems to handle as many as one hundred slides or 30,000 frames of film with or without computer assistance. Systems may include special projectors or may incorporate standard projection devices and multiple remote control of one projector or control of dual projectors from one station is possible. Some units are available that attach directly to standard slide projectors with no modifications, offering a substantial cost savings by utilizing in-inventory projectors.

Random access devices features are categorized in *data group 18b.* In addition to this data grouping, random access capabilities exist in certain audio tape recorders and microform devices, data groups 4 and 8 respectively.

Random access devices on the market have been evaluated with respect to the following features:

- Lens Type
    - Zoom Lens Available
    - Assorted Lenses Available

- Illumination
    - Conventional Lamp
    - Hi-Intensity Lamp (designed for front projection in lighted rooms)

- Visual Display
    - 2 inch x 2 inch Slides
    - Super 8mm film
    - 16mm film
    - 35mm loop

- Presentation Characteristics
    - Audio Capability
    - Limiting Search Interval (Maximum time required during a presentation for search)
        - 3.5 seconds
        - 4.0 seconds
        - 4.5 seconds
        - 5.5 seconds
        - 6.0 seconds
        - 7.0 seconds
        - 8.3 seconds
        - 15.0 seconds
        - 9 minutes
        - 13.3 minutes

    - Average Search Interval (Average search time required during a presentation)
        - 2.0 seconds
        - 2.3 seconds
        - 2.5 seconds
        - 3.0 seconds
        - 4.1 seconds
        - 5.0 seconds
        - 6.1 seconds
        - 7.0 seconds

- Operating Characteristics
    - Dual Projector Control Option Available
    - Multiple Control of Projector Option Available
    - Remote Control of Operations (varies from only frame selection to include Forward, Reverse On-Off as well as Focus)
    - Built-in Programming Capability
    - Portable

- Machine Capacity
    - up to 40 frames
    - 48 frames
    - up to 80 frames
    - 96 frames
    - 100 frames
    - 140 frames
    - 500 frames
    - 30,000 frames

Responders

Student responders serve to complete the student to teacher portion of the communication loop by enabling the acquisition of real-time or delayed response data. Responders provide the ability to test each student's comprehension during or after learning and to evaluate the performance of each student or student group.

The category "Responders" can be divided into three separate subcategories. The first is comprised of *individualized* response devices or methods which do not control presentation media. (Individualized devices having media control are subsumed in the category "Teaching Machines.") The second consists of student *group* response systems which are manually operated and have no media control. The third is comprised of student *group* response systems that have the capability to control presentations and have an automated mode of operation.

Individualized responders such as the written, oral or practical test are best suited to elicit a constructed response. The oral or written response may be either specific* or created.* The instructor's preference should be stated in the test question. Performance as a constructed response is the most time consuming to evaluate, since each student in a group must be evaluated separately. An oral test, such as a "quiz for understanding" question during a lecture, might be responded to through the use of a hand-held answer cube or answer card. The cube or card has printed surfaces which state multiple choice answers such as TRUE, FALSE, NEITHER, BOTH, A, B, C, D, DON'T UNDERSTAND or REPEAT. This type of responder will insure total class participation during a quiz but its use is limited due to reduced visibility with greater distance caused by large groups.

Some individualized response devices are designed to accept standard data processing cards which are "hole punched" each time a response is made. One such device has the capability of advancing after each correct response and can be adjusted for various 2, 3, or 4 choice answer codes. The device thus provides evaluative feedback.

Group Responders without Presentation Control can satisfy large group requirements. A basic group response system is an easy-to-operate mechanized communication system between the instructor and his students. It consists of an instructor unit and student responders. The instructor unit consists of sets of indicator lamps, meters or counters for each student position in the system. Each student's responder has a set of switches which correspond to correct-answer choices during multiple choice testing. When the instructor has finished asking or displaying the question, the student is directed to respond by selecting the switch that corresponds to his choice of correct answer. By monitoring the display on his console, the instructor can see which of the students are responding and their choice of answer. Student reinforcement is added to some systems by placing a correct answer light at the student responder, with a corresponding control switch at the instructor's station. This feature provides informative and sometimes evaluative feedback. Using more sophisticated systems, the teacher can assign a point value to each question. As questions are asked and responses given, students responding correctly are credited electronically, with the assigned point value. The accumulated scores are totaled and displayed by console-mounted counters. Some systems

---

*Definitions of these terms are given in Chapter 1.

monitor group performance through the use of meters. Each meter indicates the percentage of the class that selected each of the multiple choice answers. At a glance, the teacher can evaluate the effectiveness of his presentation to the entire group by checking the meters. Another method for displaying answer distribution is the light bar display. As the students make their answer choices, the answer distribution light bars show the proportion of the class that selects each of the possible multiple choice answers. As answers are changed, the light bars immediately register any change in proportional distribution.

Data printers are available for hard copy printout of the following student response information (which varies with system design):

- Course identification
- Student identification
- Question number
- Specific student response choice
- No answer indicator
- Assigned response weight
- Number of students responding
- The percent of students responding A, B, C, and D
- The total score for each student

Another type of permanent record is the Group Profile Recorder, which provides, on a single sheet of paper, a printed record of the responses made by the entire class. A printed chart record is geometrically arranged so that individual students and the class as a group may be evaluated with ease. Some recorders have two operating modes:

- Record only the response of students who have answered correctly
- Record all correct and incorrect answers of all students

Group Responders with Presentation Control have the capability of automated operation and are the most sophisticated systems in the responder category. Manual or automatic remote control of devices which can be operated electrically, such as video tape players, motion or still picture projectors, and room lighting, is characteristic of these large group systems. Automated operation is accomplished by a control program recorded on magnetic tape. The program controls the presentation and the processing of student responses.

In typical use, an instructional unit is presented using either a motion picture or still projector or both, together with audio from the motion film sound-track or the control tape. After a portion of the instructional unit has been presented, a tape command would cause a display of questions and possible answers. The next program operation would be to record the response of each student. Correct answer information is then presented after which the next portion of the instructional unit is begun.

Some systems are modular in design. This allows the user to build his system to satisfy immediate needs and still have the capability to expand. Modular systems can be expanded to meet increased student loading and the requirement for more complex operations.

Responders on the market are categorized in *data group 18c* and have been evaluated with respect to the following features:

- Displays
  - Group response per question in percentage
  - Group response per question
  - Student cumulative score
  - Student cumulative score in percentage
  - Weight and answer per question
  - Student identification by name
  - Minimal student
  - Response distribution, remote

- Recording Capability
  - Right answer indication
  - Specific wrong answer
  - No answer indication
  - Raw score per question
  - Student identification by number
  - Student identification by name
  - Student total raw score
  - Student percent score

- Maximum Student Load Capability
  - Up to 240
  - Up to 150
  - Up to 100
  - Up to 60
  - Up to 50
  - Up to 30
  - Up to 15
  - Up to 10
  - Single student use

- Type of Computer Compatibility
  - Punched card
  - Punched tape
  - Magnetic tape
  - Electrical interface

- Type of Response
  - Multiple Choice
  - Constructed, written
  - Constructed, spoken
  - Constructed, demonstrated

- Type of Response "freeze" control
  - Automated
  - Manual
  - Timer

- General Features

    Self contained programming capability
    Confidential response
    Automated operation, audio/visual
    Automated operation, question and answer
    Student reinforcement capability
    Manual media control
    Response weighting
    Modular system
    Right answers give electrical closure signal

PART THREE
SPECIFIC DEVICE SELECTION

Instructional Device Master List

This section of the book lists the various features available on each device associated with the generic media described in Part II. After the generic media type candidates have been selected via the Media Capabilities Matrix, the Generic Media Section of the book should be consulted to obtain a detailed description of the candidate medium and its capabilities as well as the available features. The specific devices which have the desired features can then be isolated by using the Instructional Device Master List (IDML) that follows (see Figure 3).

The IDML contains the following information:

- Data Group Number   This corresponds to the number of the chapter in which the principal discussion of this group is written.

- Device Category   The name of the group.

- Feature Number   The identifying number of each feature in each group. These numbers are the same as the column leading numbers in the list itself.

- Feature Name

- Machine Number   The identifying number of each device in the group. The model and manufacturer of each device are identified by this number in the device index.

- Feature Listing   A matrix in which the rows correspond to a particular device and the columns correspond to the particular features of this data group. The numeral 1 at any interaction indicates that the device represented by that row has the feature represented by that column.

- Price Code (P/C)   A set of letters indicating the range of prices into which the device price falls as quoted by the manufacturer. In general, the quoted price includes all features including options which are indicated in the feature listing. These price ranges are intended only as a general guide and are subject to change, discount, and negotiation. The code letters are as follows:

A—less than $10

B—less than $25 but greater than $10

C—less than $50 but greater than $25

D—less than $75 but greater than $50

E—less than $100 but greater than $75

F—less than $250 but greater than $100

G—less than $500 but greater than $250

H—less than $750 but greater than $500

J—less than $1000 but greater than $750

K—less than $2500 but greater than $1000

L—less than $5000 but greater than $2500

M—less than $7500 but greater than $5000

N—less than $10,000 but greater than $7500

P—less than $25,000 but greater than $10,000

Q—less than $50,000 but greater than $25,000

R—less than $75,000 but greater than $50,000

S—less than $100,000 but greater than $75,000

T—greater than $100,000

X—custom installation, wide price variance

Manual selection of a training device incorporating those features desired can be accomplished by tracking individual feature numbers (see Figure 3 for a hypothetical case). This tracking can be aided through the use of the Data Locator (Figure 4) placed under the column heading numbers on the Data Group sheet. A pencil mark is placed on the Data Locator edge directly above each heading number corresponding to the features of interest.* It can then be moved down the list and each line scanned for a "1" above each mark. Where correspondence is found between the "1"s on the page and the pencil marks on the Data Locator, the machine number should be noted. The remaining "1"s in that row indicate additional features and capabilities available on that device. These additional features and the pricing information can be an aid to selection when more than one device is found with the desired features.

The data contained in this book can be accessed automatically, of course, if placed into an electronic digital computer—as done originally by the authors. While convenient, automatic processing will provide no further information than can be obtained using the manual method described above and illustrated in Figure 3.

A facsimile of the Data Locator (Figure 4) is found on Page 189, immediately following this book's References page. A plastic Data Locator is found in the packet attached to the back inside cover of this book.

---

*A plain sheet of paper may be used instead of the Data Locator, using the "characteristics" column headings as a reference for placing the pencil marks. Marks should then also be made over the "machine number" and "p/c" columns to aid in maintaining alignment of the paper.

INSTRUCTIONAL DEVICE MASTER LIST

DATA GROUP 7b   DEVICE CATEGORY   8MM/SUPER 8MM MOTION PICTURE PROJECTORS

FEATURE NO	FEATURE NAME
01	ZOOM LENS AVAILABLE
02	SINGLE FIXED LENS
03	ASSORTED LENSES AVAILABLE
04	OPTICAL SOUND TRACK
05	MAGNETIC SOUND TRACK
06	CASSETTE MAGNETIC TAPE SOUND TRACK
07	RECORDING CAPABILITY
08	REEL TO REEL FILM LOADING
09	CARTRIDGE FILM LOADING
10	FILM FORMAT SUPER 8MM
11	FILM FORMAT REGULAR 8MM
12	CONTINUOUS LOOP CARTRIDGE LOADING
13	CAPACITY UP TO 50 FEET
14	CAPACITY UP TO 100 FEET
15	CAPACITY UP TO 200 FEET
16	CAPACITY UP TO 300 FEET
17	CAPACITY UP TO 400 FEET
18	CAPACITY UP TO 600 FEET
19	CAPACITY UP TO 800 FEET
20	CAPACITY UP TO 1200 FEET
21	VARIABLE SPEED SLOW MOTION
22	SINGLE FRAME/STILL CAPABILITY
23	AUTOMATIC THREADING
24	BUILT-IN REAR PROJECTION
25	FRONT PROJECTION
26	REMOTE CONTROL
27	MIXED MOTION/STILL CAPABILITY
28	REMOTE SPEAKER
29	BUILT-IN SPEAKER
30	SILENT SPEED 18 FPS
31	SOUND SPEED 24 FPS

THESE DESIRED FEATURES ARE FOUND IN THESE COLUMNS

MACHINE NO   CHARACTERISTICS

MACHINE NO: 001, 002, 003, 004, 005, 006, 007, 008, 009, 010, 011, 012, 013, 014, 015, 016, 017, 018, 019, 020

INDICATING THESE MACHINES

THE DATA GROUP 7b INDEX SHOWS MACHINE 002 TO BE THE BOHN BENTON INSTITOR AND 013 TO BE THE FAIRCHILD MODEL 711

P/C

PRICE RANGE FOR MODEL WITH ALL LISTED OPTIONS

BETWEEN $250 & $500
BETWEEN $500 & $750

Figure 3

Sample Machine Selection

Device Index

DATA GROUP 3   DEVICE CATEGORY   OVERHEAD PROJECTORS

FEATURE NO   FEATURE NAME

Feature No	Feature Name
01	TABLE TOP
02	FLOOR MODEL
03	CARRY CASE
04	WEIGHT - LESS THAN 10 LBS
05	WEIGHT - LESS THAN 15 LBS
06	WEIGHT - LESS THAN 20 LBS
07	WEIGHT - LESS THAN 30 LBS
08	WEIGHT - LESS THAN 40 LBS
09	--------------------
10	INCANDESCENT LAMP
11	QUARTZ-HALOGEN OR TUNGSTEN-HALOGEN LAMP
12	RATED LAMP LIFE UP TO 2000 HRS
13	RATED LAMP LIFE UP TO 600 HRS
14	RATED LAMP LIFE UP TO 500 HRS
15	RATED LAMP LIFE UP TO 75 HRS
16	RATED LAMP LIFE UP TO 50 HRS
17	RATED LAMP LIFE UP TO 25 HRS
18	HI/LO ILLUMINATION CONTROL
19	LAMP CHANGE AUTOMATIC
20	LAMP CHANGE SEMI-AUTOMATIC
21	LAMP EJECTOR
22	CONDENSER SYSTEM
23	CONDENSER AND FRESNEL LENS
24	FRESNEL LENS
25	AUTOMATIC OVER-TEMP CUTOFF
26	AUTOMATIC FAN SHUT OFF DELAY
27	GLARE SHIELD
28	NON-GLARE STAGE
29	SPARE LAMP STORAGE
30	SPARE LAMP IN USE INDICATOR
31	WRITING ROLL
32	BUILT-IN SLIDE PROJECTION
33	SIMULTANEOUS SLIDE/TRANSPARENCY
34	MICROSWITCH DOWSER
35	BUILT-IN LENS SELECTION
36	STAGE TEMPERATURE NO GREATER THAN 100 DEGREES
37	POWER FOCUS
38	2X2 SLIDE ADAPTER AT EXTRA COST
39	ASSORTED LENSES AVAILABLE
40	360 DEGREE SWIVEL HEAD
41	FOLD-AWAY PORTABLE
42	EXTRA-WIDE ANGLE LENS (10 1/2 INCH FOCAL LENGTH)

MACHINE NO   CHARACTERISTICS   P/C

```
                0000000001111_11111222222222233333333334444444444555555555556
                1234567890123456789012345678901234567890123456789012345678901234567890
```

Machine No	Characteristics	P/C
001	1 1 1 1 11 1 1 1	G
002	1 1 111 1 111 1 1 1 1	F
003	1 111 1 111 11 1 1 111	F
004	1 111 1 111 11 1 1 111 1	F
005	1 1 111 1 111 1 1 1 1 1 1	F
006	1 111 1 111 1 11 11 1 1 1 1	F
007	1 1 111 1 111 11 1 11 1 1 1	F
008	1 111 1 111 11 1 1 1 1	G
009	1 111 1 111 11 1 1 1 1 1	G
010	1 1 1 1 111 11 1 11 111 1	F
011	1 11 1 111 1 1 1	G
012	1 1 1 111 1 1 1 1	F
013	1 1 11 1 111 1 1 1	G
014	1 1 11 1 11111 1 11 1	
015		G
016	1 1 111 1 1111 1 1 1 1 1 1 1 1	
017		G
018	1 111 1 111 1 1 1 1 1	K
019	1 1 11 1 1 111	K
020	1 1 111 1 1 1	G
021	1 1 11 1 111 1 1 1 1 111 1	G
022	1 111111 1 111 1 1	F
023	1 111 1 111 1 1 1 111 1	G
024	1 11 1 111 1 1 1	

DATA GROUP 3   DEVICE CATEGORY   OVERHEAD PROJECTORS

(continued)

P/C   H F G G F G F F G G F F F

MACHINE NO   CHARACTERISTICS

```
              00000000011111111112222222222333333333344444444445555555556
              12345678901234567890123456789012345678901234567890123456789
0
025           1    1    1           1         1         1
026           1   111   1           1   1     1              1
027           1   111  111   1      11       11   1
028           1   111  1      1     11    1   11       1           1
029           1    11   1     1      1    1   111
030           1   111  111         111    11  11       1      1
031           1   111  111    11   111    11  111   11
032           1   111  111    11   111    11  111   11
033           1   111  111    1    111    11  111      11     11
034           1   111  111    1    111    11  111      11
035           1   111  111    1    111    11  111      1   1  1
036           1   1111 111    1    111    11  111      11     11  1
037           1   1111 111    1    111    11  111      11     11  1
```

DATA GROUP 4   DEVICE CATEGORY   MAGNETIC TAPE AUDIO RECORDERS

FEATURE NO	FEATURE NAME
01	REEL TO REEL LOADING
02	CASSETTE LOADING
03	CONTINUOUS LOOP CARTRIDGE LOADING
04	MONAURAL AUDIO
05	STEREO AUDIO
06	STEREO FORMAT 2 TRACK
07	STEREO FORMAT 4 TRACK
08	STEREO FORMAT 8 TRACK
09	MONAURAL FORMAT QUARTER TRACK
10	MONAURAL FORMAT HALF TRACK
11	MONAURAL FORMAT FULL TRACK
12	MONAURAL FORMAT MULTI-TRACK
13	RECORDING CAPABILITY
14	PLAYBACK CAPABILITY
15	RANDOM ACCESSING
16	SPEAKER/HEADSET OUTPUT
17	LOW LEVEL INPUT - MICROPHONE
18	HIGH LEVEL INPUT - RADIO/PHONO
19	INTERNAL SPEAKER
20	EXTERNAL SPEAKER/HEAD SET REQUIRED
21	117 VAC POWER
22	BATTERY POWER
23	PORTABLE
24	AUTOMATIC SHUT OFF
25	FULL REMOTE CONTROL
26	REMOTE PAUSE VIA MIKE SWITCH
27	REMOTE PAUSE VIA FOOT CONTROL
28	STUDENT RECORD TRACK
29	1-7/8 IPS SPEED
30	3-3/4 IPS SPEED
31	7-1/2 IPS SPEED
32	15 IPS SPEED
33	BUILT-IN REPEAT/REVIEW
34	AUTOMATIC TAPE REVERSAL
35	AUTOMATIC STOP FOR STUDENT ACTION

MACHINE NO   CHARACTERISTICS

```
          0000000001111111111222222222233333333334444444444555555555 6
          1234567890123456789012345678901234567890123456789012345678 90
001
002
003
004
005
006
007
008
009
010
011
012
013
014
015
016
017
018
019
020
021
022
023
024
025
026
027
028
029
030
031
```

DATA GROUP 4 DEVICE CATEGORY   MAGNETIC TAPE AUDIO RECORDERS

(continued)

P/C

MACHINE NO   CHARACTERISTICS

```
          00000000011111111112222222222333333333344444444445555555556
          12345678901234567890123456789012345678901234567890123456789
```

032
033
034
035
036
037
038
039
040
041
042
043
044
045
046
047
048
049
050
051
052
053
054
055
056
057
058
059
060
061
062
063
064
065
066
067
068
069
070
071
072
073
074
075
076
077
078
079
080
081
082
083
084
085
086
087
088
089
090

INSTRUCTIONAL DEVICE MASTER LIST

DATA GROUP 5   DEVICE CATEGORY   2X2 SLIDE AND SOUND SLIDE PROJECTORS

FEATURE NO	FEATURE NAME
01	ZOOM LENS AVAILABLE
02	SINGLE FIXED LENS
03	ASSORTED LENSES AVAILABLE
04	CONVENTIONAL LAMP
05	HIGH INTENSITY LAMP
06	REEL TO REEL AUDIO TAPE
07	CASSETTE AUDIO TAPE
08	REVERSE SYNCHRONIZATION OF AUDIO
09	SOUND-SLIDE DEVICE
10	BUILT-IN RECORD CAPABILITY
11	SLIDE CAPACITY UP TO 12
12	SLIDE CAPACITY UP TO 36
13	SLIDE CAPACITY UP TO 48
14	SLIDE CAPACITY UP TO 50
15	SLIDE CAPACITY UP TO 80
16	SLIDE CAPACITY UP TO 96
17	SLIDE CAPACITY-Y UP TO 100
18	SLIDE CAPACITY-Y UP TO 120
19	SLIDE CAPACITY-Y UP TO 140
20	REMOTE CONTROL-ELECTRICAL
21	BUILT-IN REAR PROJECTION
22	FRONT PROJECTION
23	BUILT-IN PROGRAMMER
24	AUTOMATIC TIMED OPERATION
25	PORTABLE
26	FILM-STRIP OPTION
27	PREVIEWER
28	CARTRIDGE SLIDE LOADING
29	CARTRIDGE AUDIO TAPE

MACHINE NO   CHARACTERISTICS

```
                    0000000001111111111222222222233333333334444444444555555555 6
                    1234567890123456789012345678901234567890123456789012345678 90
001
002
003
004
005
006
007
008
009
010
011
012
013
014
015
016
017
018
019
020
021
022
023
024
025
026
027
028
029
030
031
032
033
034
035
036
037
```

DATA GROUP 5 **DEVICE CATEGORY   2X2 SLIDE AND SOUND SLIDE PROJECTORS**

(continued)   **MACHINE NO   CHARACTERISTICS**   P/C

```
0000000001111111111222222222233333333334444444444555555555 6
1234567890123456789012345678901234567890123456789012345678 90
```

MACHINE NO	CHARACTERISTICS (columns 01–58)	P/C
038	`1 1 1  11111 1111   1 1111`	G
039	`1 1  1 111111111    1 1111`	G
040	`1 1  1 111111       11 11`	K
041	`1 1  1 1111111      11 11`	L
042	`1 1  1 1 111111     11  1`	K
043	`1  1    111111      1 1111`	H
044	`1 1     11111       1 1111`	H
045		
046		
047	`1 1  1 1 11111111111   1`	K
048	`1 11  1 1 11111111111 1 11`	G
049	`1 1  1 111111       11 1111`	G
050	`1 1  1 111111111111 1111`	G
051	`1  1      11         1 1 11   1`	F
052	`1 1 1     11111      1 1 1`	K
053	`1 1       11111      1 1 1`	K
054	`1 1     1 1111111    11  1      1`	G

INSTRUCTIONAL DEVICE MASTER LIST

DATA GROUP 6a DEVICE CATEGORY FILMSTRIP PROJECTORS

FEATURE NO	FEATURE NAME
01	ZOOM LENS AVAILABLE
02	SINGLE FIXED LENS
03	ASSORTED LENSES AVAILABLE
04	
05	2X2 SLIDE CAPABILITY
06	CONTINUOUS LOOP CAPABILITY
07	DOUBLE FRAME FILMSTRIP CAPABILITY
08	FRONT PROJECTION
09	BUILT-IN REAR PROJECTION
10	REMOTE CONTROL
11	BATTERY OPERATION
12	BUILT-IN POINTER

P/C

FF FFFCFFFWWFFWWFFFCFCCWFFFWWFFCC BBCCWBBBBBDCFCBF

MACHINE NO CHARACTERISTICS

0000000001111111111222222222233333333334444444444555555555 6
1234567890123456789012345678901234567890123456789012345678 90

001
002
003
004
005
006
007
008
009
010
011
012
013
014
015
016
017
018
019
020
021
022
023
024
025
026
027
028
029
030
031
032
033
034
035
036
037
038
039
040
041
042
043
044
045
046
047

INSTRUCTIONAL DEVICE MASTER LIST

DATA GROUP 6b DEVICE CATEGORY   SOUND FILMSTRIP PROJECTORS

FEATURE NO   FEATURE NAME

01   SINGLE FIXED LENS
02   ASSORTED LENSES AVAILABLE
03   DISK SPEED 16-2/3 RPM
04   DISK SPEED 33-1/3 RPM
05   DISK SPEED 45 RPM
06   DISK SPEED 78 RPM
07   TAPE SPEED 1-7/8 IPS
08   TAPE SPEED 3-3/4 IPS
09   RECORD CAPABILITY
10   35MM FILMSTRIP
11   CONTINUOUS LOOP
12   2X2 SLIDE CAPABILITY
13   8MM/SUPER 8MM
14   16MM
15   DOUBLE-FRAME FILMSTRIP
16   FRONT PROJECTION
17   BUILT-IN REAR PROJECTION
18   BUILT-IN SPEAKER
19   REMOTE SPEAKER
---
20   REMOTE CONTROL
21   PROGRAM HOLD
22
23   BUILT IN FRONT PROJECTION SCREEN

MACHINE NO   CHARACTERISTICS

P/C   GGGGFFFFFFGGGGFDFEGGGGGGFGFFGG FGFFFFFFFGGGG

                00C00000011111111112222222222333333333344444444445555555556
                12345678901234567890123456789012345678901234567890123456789012345678901234567890

001
002
003
004
005
006
007
008
009
010
011
012
013
014
015
016
017
018
019
020
021
022
023
024
025
026
027
028
029
030
031
032
033
034
035
036
037
038
039
040
041
042
043

DATA GROUP 6b DEVICE CATEGORY   SOUND FILMSTRIP PROJECTORS

(continued)

MACHINE NO   CHARACTERISTICS

P/C F F F F F F F G G G G G F F G

```
                0000000000111111111122222222223333333333444444444455555555556
                1234567890123456789012345678901234567890123456789012345678 90
044
045
046
047
048
049
050
051
052
053
054
055
056
057
```

INSTRUCTIONAL DEVICE MASTER LIST

DATA GROUP 7a   DEVICE CATEGORY   16MM PROJECTORS

P/C

FEATURE NO	FEATURE NAME
01	ZOOM LENS AVAILABLE
02	SINGLE FIXED LENS
03	ASSORTED LENSES AVAILABLE
04	OPTICAL SOUND TRACK
05	MAGNETIC SOUND TRACK
06	RECORDING CAPABILITY
07	REEL TO REEL LOADING
08	CONTINUOUS LOOP CARTRIDGE LOADING
09	SLOW MOTION CAPABILITY
10	SOUND SPEED 24 FPS
11	SILENT SPEED 18 FPS
12	STILL PICTURE/SINGLE FRAME CAPABILITY
13	CAPACITY UP TO 800 FEET
14	CAPACITY UP TO 1000 FEET
15	CAPACITY UP TO 1200 FEET
16	CAPACITY UP TO 1600 FEET
17	CAPACITY UP TO 2000 FEET
18	CAPACITY UP TO 2200 FEET
19	CAPACITY UP TO 2400 FEET
20	CAPACITY UP TO 4000 FEET
21	CAPACITY UP TO 5000 FEET
22	CAPACITY UP TO 7000 FEET
23	AUTOMATIC THREADING
24	REMOTE CONTROL
25	BUILT-IN REAR PROJECTION
26	FRONT PROJECTION
27	BUILT-IN SPEAKER
28	REMOTE SPEAKER
29	REQUIRES SEPARATE AMPLIFIER
30	HIGH-INTENSITY LAMP
31	CONVENTIONAL LAMP
32	PORTABLE
33	FAST FORWARD TO SELECTED LOCATION

MACHINE NO   CHARACTERISTICS

```
          0000000001111111111222222222233333333334444444444555555555 6
          1234567890123456789012345678901234567890123456789012345678 90
001
002
003
004
005
006
007
008
009
010
011
012
013
014
015
016
017
018
019
020
021
022
023
024
025
026
027
028
029
030
031
032
033
```

INSTRUCTIONAL DEVICE MASTER LIST

DATA GROUP 7a DEVICE CATEGORY   16MM PROJECTORS

(continued)

MACHINE NO   CHARACTERISTICS

P/C

```
          0000000001111111111222222222233333333334444444444555555555566
          1234567890123456789012345678901234567890123456789012345678901234567890
```

034
035
036
037
038
039
040
041
042
043
044
045
046
047
048
049
050
051
052
053
054
055
056
057
058
059
060
061
062
063
064
065
066
067
068
069
070
071
072
073
074
075
076
077
078
079
080
081
082
083

DATA GROUP 7b **DEVICE CATEGORY** 8MM/SUPER 8MM MOTION PICTURE PROJECTORS

FEATURE NO	FEATURE NAME
01	ZOOM LENS AVAILABLE
02	SINGLE FIXED LENS
03	ASSORTED LENSES AVAILABLE
04	OPTICAL SOUND TRACK
05	MAGNETIC SOUND TRACK
06	CASSETTE MAGNETIC TAPE SOUND TRACK
07	RECORDING CAPABILITY
08	REEL TO REEL FILM LOADING
09	CARTRIDGE FILM LOADING
10	FILM FORMAT SUPER 8MM
11	FILM FORMAT REGULAR 8MM
12	CONTINUOUS LOOP CARTRIDGE LOADING
13	CAPACITY UP TO 50 FEET
14	CAPACITY UP TO 100 FEET
15	CAPACITY UP TO 200 FEET
16	CAPACITY UP TO 300 FEET
17	CAPACITY UP TO 400 FEET
18	CAPACITY UP TO 600 FEET
19	CAPACITY UP TO 800 FEET
20	CAPACITY UP TO 1200 FEET
21	VARIABLE SPEED SLOW MOTION
22	SINGLE FRAME/STILL CAPABILITY
23	AUTOMATIC THREADING
24	BUILT-IN REAR PROJECTION
25	FRONT PROJECTION
26	REMOTE CONTROL
27	MIXED MOTION/STILL CAPABILITY
28	REMOTE SPEAKER
29	BUILT-IN SPEAKER
30	SILENT SPEED 18 FPS
31	SOUND SPEED 24 FPS
32	SLOW MOTION 6 FPS
33	SLOW MOTION 8 FPS
34	NOTE - ACTUAL CAPACITY 50 FEET HALF-HOUR PROGRAM CAN BE
35	EQUIVALENT TO 400 FEET
36	ACCELERATED PROJECTION SPEED 54FPS
37	AUTOMATIC FILM CARTRIDGE CHANGING

MACHINE NO   CHARACTERISTICS   P/C

```
            0000000001111111111222222222233333333334444444444555555555 6
            1234567890123456789012345678901234567890123456789012345678 90
```

MACHINE NO	CHARACTERISTICS	P/C
001	`1    1 11 1  1111111   1 1    111`	G
002	`11  1   11 111111      1111    1 1`	G
003	`1   111 1   11111      1 11    11`	F
004	` 1  1   11 111         11 1    1 1`	H
005	`1 11 11 1   111111    11 11 1   11`	F
006	`   1   1 1  11111     11 111   11      1`	F
007	`1  1  1 1   111        1 1    111`	F
0C8	`1    11  11            11 1    1`	H
009	` 1  1 11 1  11111111      1    111`	G
010	`1   1 11 11 111111        1    111`	F
011	`11  1 11 1   111111       1    111`	
012		
013	`1    1 1111  11111      1 11   1 1`	H
014	`1  1 1 11 111111       11 1    1 1`	H
015	`1  1 1 11 111111       1      1 1`	J
016	`1  1 1 11 111111         1    1 1`	F
017	`1     1 11 111111      11 1    111`	G
018	`1    111111111111      11 1    11`	F
019	`1     1 11 11111       1 1    1111`	H
020	`1  1 11 11 11111       1 1   111111`	G
021	`11 11  1 11 1111111    11 1   1111`	G
022	`1   1 1  1 11111111    1 1    1 1`	F
023	`11    11 11           111    1`	H
024	` 1  1 1111 11111          11  111`	G
025	`1   1  11   11111     1111  1 1111111`	G
026	`11  1 11 1  1111111    1 1   1111`	F
027	`11     1 1   11111     1 1    1`	
028		
029		

DATA GROUP 7b DEVICE CATEGORY 8MM/SUPER 8MM MOTION PICTURE PROJECTORS

(continued)

MACHINE NO   CHARACTERISTICS   P/C

```
          0000000001111111111222222222233333333334444444444555555555 6
          1234567890123456789012345678901234567890123456789012345 67890

030
031
032                    11 11           111 1        1
033
034                    11  111111111     11  111      111  1
035         1  1        11  111111111    111  111      11   11
036         1  1   1     1  11  1 111     111  1 111
037
038         1         1   1  111111      111 111 11     111 1
039         1  1       11  1111111       111 111 111    1111 11
040        11  1       1  11  111         1  1  1
041         11 1       11  111111111    111   1  1      11 1 1
042         111 1      11  111111111     11  11  1      1111
043         111 1      11  111111111     1   1  1       11 1
044
045         1  1       11  11111111      111  1          111 1
046
047         1  1   1   11   11111         1    1
048         11111      1111 11111111    111  111 1      1111
049         11111      1111 111111111   111  111 1      1111
050         1  1   1   11  11  1 11       1    1          111  1
051         111111     11111111111111    111  111        111
052         11  1      111 111111        111  1 1        1  1
053         11  1      111 11111         111  1 1       1111 1
054         11         111  1 11         1    1          11  1
055         111        11   1 11        111   11         11 1
056         111        11   1  1        111   1 1        11 1      1
057         1  1        1   1  1          1  1 1
058
```

DATA GROUP 8   DEVICE CATEGORY   MICROFORM DEVICES

FEATURE NO	FEATURE NAME
01	MICROFILM
02	MICROFICHE
03	APERTURE CARDS
04	COM FICHE
05	35MM ROLL FILM
06	35MM STRIPS
07	MICRO-JACKETS
08	REAR SCREEN PROJECTION
09	FRONT PROJECTION
10	117 VAC
11	BATTERY POWER
12	PORTABLE
13	INDEX METHOD EAR CODING
14	INDEX METHOD STYLUS
15	INDEX METHOD COUNTER
16	INDEX METHOD MANUAL X-Y SEARCH
17	MAGNIFICATION VARIABLE
18	MAGNIFICATION FIXED
19	-----
20	FIXED SCREEN SIZE
21	OPTIONAL SCREEN SIZES AVAILABLE
22	-----
23	MAGAZINE LOAD
24	RANDOM ACCESSING
25	CARTRIDGE LOAD

MACHINE NO   CHARACTERISTICS

```
          0000000001111111111222222222233333333334444444444555555555 6
          1234567890123456789012345678901234567890123456789012345678 0

P/C       E F  G G I F F D J G I K G M J P F F L D B M M K

001
002
003
004
005
006
007
008
009
010
011
012
013
014
015
016
017
018
019
020
021
022
023
024
025
026
027
```

INSTRUCTIONAL DEVICE MASTER LIST

DATA GROUP 9   DEVICE CATEGORY   TEACHING MACHINES

FEATURE NO   FEATURE NAME

01   INDIVIDUAL STUDENT UNIT
02   MULTIPLE CHOICE RESPONSE
03   CONSTRUCTED RESPONSE
04   STUDENT REINFORCEMENT
05   RESPONSE COUNTER
06   PERMANENT RECORD
07   MOTION VISUAL
08   STILL VISUAL
09   AUDIO
10   CASSETTE
11   CARTRIDGE
12   RESPONSE CONTROLLED MEDIA
13   MANUAL CONTROL OF MEDIA
14   WILL CONTROL EXTERNAL MEDIA
15   16MM FILM
16   2X2 SLIDE
17   FILM STRIP
18   MAGNETIC AUDIO TAPE
19   AUDIO PRESSED DISC
20   DESK TOP UNIT
21   HAND PORTABLE
22   MODULARIZED SYSTEM
23   CARREL CONFIGURATION
24   COMPUTER COMPATIBLE
25   ADAPTIVE PROGRAM
26   LINEAR PROGRAM
27   BRANCHED PROGRAM
28   STUDENT SELF PACING
29   MACHINE PACING
30   CUSTOMIZED PROGRAM REQUIRED
31   SELF CONTAINED PROGRAMMING
32   MANUFACTURER FORMAT
33   RANDOM ACCESS INFORMATION RETRIEVAL

MACHINE NO   CHARACTERISTICS

```
        0000000001111111111222222222233333333334444444444555555555 6
        1234567890123456789012345678901234567890123456789012345678 90

001
002
003
004
005
006
007
008
009
010
011
012
013
014
015
016
017
018
019
020
021
022
023
024
025
026
```

DATA GROUP 10a DEVICE CATEGORY   VIDEO TAPE RECORDERS AND PLAYERS

FEATURE NO	FEATURE NAME
01	RECORD AND PLAY
02	RECORD ONLY
03	PLAY ONLY
04	MONOCHROME
05	COLOR
06	COLOR ADAPTER AVAILABLE AT ADDED COST
07	1 INCH TAPE
08	1/2 INCH TAPE
09	-----
11	-----
12	-----
13	-----
14	-----
15	-----
16	-----
17	-----
18	-----
19	SLOW MOTION CAPABILITY
20	VARIABLE MOTION CAPABILITY
21	STOP ACTION CAPABILITY
22	REMOTE CONTROL
23	ELECTRONIC EDITING CAPABILITY
24	FCC STANDARD ELECTRONIC EDITING
25	PLAYING TIME UP TO 420 MINUTES SLOW SCAN RATE
26	PLAYING TIME UP TO 60 MINUTES
27	PLAYING TIME UP TO 40 MINUTES
28	PLAYING TIME UP TO 30 MINUTES
29	TAPE SPEED 9-5 IPS
30	TAPE SPEED 7-5 IPS
31	TAPE SPEED 8-57 IPS
32	TAPE SPEED 7-8 IPS
33	TAPE SPEED 1.0625 IPS
34	MANUFACTURERS FORMAT
35	EIAJ TYPE ONE FORMAT
36	-----
37	-----
38	SUIT CASE PORTABLE
39	TIME LAPSE RECORDING
40	-----
41	-----
42	PLAYING TIME UP TO 210 MINUTES
43	TAPE REEL 12-1/2 INCH
44	TAPE REEL 7 INCH
45	TAPE REEL 8-1/2 INCH
46	TAPE REEL 9-3/4 INCH
47	TAPE REEL 10-1/2 INCH
48	TAPE SPEED 6.9 IPS
49	TAPE REEL 8 INCH
50	PLAY WHILE RECORD
51	TAPE SPEED 3-3/4 IPS
52	CASSETTE LOAD
53	-----
54	1/4 INCH TAPE
55	PLAYING TIME UP TO 120 MINUTES
56	TAPE SPEED 11.25 IPS
57	AUDIO VU METER
58	AUDIO DUBBING

MACHINE NO   CHARACTERISTICS

```
          0000000001111111111222222222233333333334444444444555555555556
          1234567890123456789012345678901234567890123456789012345678901

001       11 11                   1       1      1   1
003       1  1 1               111  1111     1 1  1  1   1
004       1  1 1               111  1111     1 1  1  1   1
005       1  1                1  1  111 1       1  1  1 1  1   1
006       1  1 1             111 1  111 1    1 1  1  1 1  1
007       1  1 1              11 1   11 1    1 1  1  1 1  1     1
```

INSTRUCTIONAL DEVICE MASTER LIST

DATA GROUP 10a DEVICE CATEGORY VIDEO TAPE RECORDERS AND PLAYERS

(continued)

MACHINE NO   CHARACTERISTICS   P/C

```
          00000000011111111112222222222333333333344444444445555555555 6
          12345678901234567890123456789012345678901234567890123456789 0

008
009
010
011
012
013
014
015
016
017
018
019
020
021
022
023
024
025
026
027
028
029
030
031
032
```

DATA GROUP 10b DEVICE CATEGORY   PORTABLE VIDEO TAPE RECORDING SYSTEMS

P/C   xxxxxxx

FEATURE NO	FEATURE NAME
01	PLAYBACK CAPABILITY
02	RF OUTPUT
03	VIDEO OUTPUT
04	MONOCHROME
05	COLOR
06	REEL TO REEL
07	CASSETTE
08	1/2 INCH TAPE
09	1/4 INCH TAPE
10	EIAJ TYPE ONE FORMAT
11	MANUFACTURER'S FORMAT
12	-----
13	RECORDING TIME UP TO 60 MINUTES
14	RECORDING TIME UP TO 40 MINUTES
15	RECORDING TIME UP TO 35 MINUTES
16	RECORDING TIME UP TO 30 MINUTES
17	RECORDING TIME UP TO 25 MINUTES
18	RECORDING TIME UP TO 20 MINUTES
19	TAPE SPEED 7.5 IPS
20	TAPE SPEED 7.9 IPS
21	TAPE SPEED 11.25 IPS
22	WEIGHT LESS THAN 35 POUNDS
23	WEIGHT LESS THAN 25 POUNDS
24	WEIGHT LESS THAN 20 POUNDS
25	ELECTRONIC VIEWFINDER
26	MECHANICAL VIEWFINDER
27	ASSORTED LENS COMPATIBILITY
28	BATTERY USAGE UP TO 80 MINUTES
29	BATTERY USAGE UP TO 60 MINUTES
30	BATTERY USAGE UP TO 40 MINUTES
31	STOP ACTION CAPABILITY
32	AUTOMATIC SEARCH
33	SOUND DUBBING
34	VIDEO EDITING CAPABILITY
35	ZOOM LENS SUPPLIED
36	SINGLE FIXED LENS SUPPLIED
37	TAPE FOOTAGE COUNTER
38	VIDEO SIGNAL LEVEL METER
39	AUDIO SIGNAL LEVEL METER
40	RECORDS FROM TV
41	117 VAC POWER
42	BATTERY POWER
43	SLOW MOTION CAPABILITY
44	BUILT-IN MONITOR
45	AUTOMATIC SHUTOFF
46	ELAPSED TIME COUNTER
47	OPTICAL VIEWFINDER
48	

MACHINE NO   CHARACTERISTICS

```
            000000000111111111122222222223333333333444444444455555555556
            123456789012345678901234567890123456789012345678901234567890
001
002
003
004
005
006
007
008
```

INSTRUCTIONAL DEVICE MASTER LIST

DATA GROUP 10c   DEVICE CATEGORY   TV MONITORS AND PROJECTORS

FEATURE NO	FEATURE NAME
01	MONITOR
02	PROJECTOR
03	COLOR
04	MONOCHROME
05	SOLID STATE ELECTRONICS
06	R.F. RECEPTION
07	UHF RECEPTION
08	VHF RECEPTION
09	CCTV INPUT
10	117 VAC 60 HZ
11	220 VAC 50 HZ
12	BATTERY POWER
13	RACK MOUNTED
14	AUDIO INPUT JACK
15	AUDIO OUTPUT JACK
16	------
17	VIDEO OUTPUT JACK
18	EXTERNAL VERTICAL SYNC INPUT
19	EXTERNAL HORIZONTAL SYNC INPUT
20	EXTENSION SPEAKER JACK
21	MULTI-DISPLAY
22	STANDBY CIRCUIT
23	VIEWING AREA 37 SQ. IN.
24	VIEWING AREA 44 SQ. IN.
25	VIEWING AREA 71 SQ. IN.
26	VIEWING AREA 88 SQ. IN.
27	VIEWING AREA 125 SQ. IN.
28	VIEWING AREA 172 SQ. IN.
29	VIEWING AREA 270 SQ. IN.
30	VIEWING AREA 282 SQ. IN.
31	VIEWING AREA 295 SQ. IN.
32	CRT 5 IN.
33	CRT 9 IN.
34	CRT 10 IN.
35	CRT 12 IN.
36	CRT 16 IN.
37	CRT 19 IN.
38	CRT 23 IN.
39	CRT 25 IN.
40	SYNC OUTPUT JACK

MACHINE NO   CHARACTERISTICS

```
            0000000000111111111122222222223333333333444444444455555555556
            1234567890123456789012345678901234567890123456789012345678901234567890
001
002
003
004
005
006
007
008
009
010
011
012
013
014
015
016
017
018
019
020
021
022
023
024
025
026
```

DATA GROUP 10c   DEVICE CATEGORY   T V MONITORS AND PROJECTORS

(continued)

MACHINE NO   CHARACTERISTICS

```
          00000000011111111112222222222333333333344444444445555555556
          12345678901234567890123456789012345678901234567890123456789 0
027       1   11   11 11 11     1             1                1
028       1 11 11111  11  1        1              1
029       1  11111   11  1       1             1
030       1   11111  1  1      1             1
031       1  111111 1
032       1 1111111
033       1 1 111111
034       1111111111
035       1 11 11111
036       1 1 11111
037       1 1 11111
038       11 11111
039       1 1 111111
```

INSTRUCTIONAL DEVICE MASTER LIST

DATA GROUP 18a DEVICE CATEGORY AUDIO VISUAL INTEGRATORS

FEATURE NO	FEATURE NAME
01	REEL TO REEL LOADING
02	CASSETTE LOADING
03	CONTINUOUS LOOP CARTRIDGE
04	SEPARATE REEL TO REEL TAPE RECORDER REQUIRED
05	SEPARATE TAPE RECORDER REQUIRED
06	CONTROL METHOD SIGNAL PULSE
07	CONTROL METHOD PENCIL MARK
08	NUMBER OF MACHINES/OPERATIONS CONTROLLABLE - AT LEAST 1
09	NUMBER OF MACHINES/OPERATIONS CONTROLLABLE - AT LEAST 2
10	NUMBER OF MACHINES/OPERATIONS CONTROLLABLE - AT LEAST 3
11	NUMBER OF MACHINES/OPERATIONS CONTROLLABLE - AT LEAST 4
12	BUILT-IN PROGRAMMING CAPABILITY
13	SPECIAL PROGRAMMING DEVICE REQUIRED
14	BUILT-IN AUDIO RECORD CAPABILITY
15	REMOTE CONTROL FEATURE
16	AUTOMATIC STOP FEATURE
17	REVERSE SYNCHRONIZATION CAPABILITY
18	ACCEPTS SIGNAL PULSE FROM EITHER TRACK

MACHINE NO   CHARACTERISTICS

(Machine numbers 001 through 037, with a matrix of binary characteristics under feature columns numbered 1–56.)

INSTRUCTIONAL DEVICE MASTER LIST

DATA GROUP 18b DEVICE CATEGORY RANDOM ACCESS DEVICES

FEATURE NO	FEATURE NAME
01	ZOOM LENS AVAILABLE
02	ASSORTED LENSES AVAILABLE
03	CONVENTIONAL LAMP
04	HIGH INTENSITY LAMP
05	2X2 SLIDES
06	SUPER 8MM
07	16MM
08	35MM CONTINUOUS LOOP
09	LIMITING SEARCH INTERVAL UP TO 3.5 SEC.
10	LIMITING SEARCH INTERVAL UP TO 4.0 SEC.
11	LIMITING SEARCH INTERVAL UP TO 4.5 SEC.
12	LIMITING SEARCH INTERVAL UP TO 5.5 SEC.
13	LIMITING SEARCH INTERVAL UP TO 6.0 SEC.
14	LIMITING SEARCH INTERVAL UP TO 7.0 SEC.
15	LIMITING SEARCH INTERVAL UP TO 8.3 SEC.
16	LIMITING SEARCH INTERVAL UP TO 9 MIN.
17	LIMITING SEARCH INTERVAL UP TO 13.3 MIN.
18	AVERAGE SEARCH INTERVAL - WIDE VARIATION
19	AVERAGE SEARCH INTERVAL UP TO 2.0 SEC.
20	AVERAGE SEARCH INTERVAL UP TO 2.3 SEC.
21	AVERAGE SEARCH INTERVAL UP TO 2.5 SEC.
22	AVERAGE SEARCH INTERVAL UP TO 3.0 SEC.
23	AVERAGE SEARCH INTERVAL UP TO 4.1 SEC.
24	AVERAGE SEARCH INTERVAL UP TO 5.0 SEC.
25	AVERAGE SEARCH INTERVAL UP TO 6.1 SEC.
26	PORTABLE
27	REMOTE CONTROL
28	LIMITING SEARCH INTERVAL UP TO 15 SEC.
29	DUAL PROJECTION OPTION AT EXTRA COST
30	MULTIPLE CONTROL OF PROJECTOR OPTION AT EXTRA COST
31	CAPACITY UP TO 48 FRAMES
32	CAPACITY UP TO 80 FRAMES
33	CAPACITY UP TO 96 FRAMES
34	CAPACITY UP TO 100 FRAMES
35	CAPACITY UP TO 140 FRAMES
36	CAPACITY UP TO 500 FRAMES
37	CAPACITY UP TO 30,000 FRAMES
38	CAPACITY UP TO 40 FRAMES
39	AUDIO CAPABILITY
40	BUILT IN PROGRAMMING CAPABILITY
41	AVERAGE SEARCH INTERVAL UP TO 7 SEC.

MACHINE NO CHARACTERISTICS

```
          000000000111111111122222222223333333333444444444455555555556
          123456789012345678901234567890123456789012345678901234567890
001       1111      1      1        11111   1
003       1111      1      11        111    1
004       1111               1      1111    1
005       11111             11      11 11111 1
006       11111            1      11 11111   1
007       11111             1       1  111   1
008       1111         11      11        1   1
009       1111         11      1 1       111111 1
010       1111              11       111111    1
011       1111              1      111111111   1
012       11 11        1          11 1111111   1
013       11 11            1       11  11111   1
014       1 111        1         1   111111   1
015       11 11        1         1    11 11   1
016       11 11        1         1    111
017       1111         1                          1111
```

INSTRUCTIONAL DEVICE MASTER LIST

DATA GROUP 18c DEVICE CATEGORY RESPONDERS

FEATURE NO	FEATURE NAME
01	DISPLAYED GROUP RESPONSE PER QUESTION IN PERCENT
02	DISPLAYED GROUP RESPONSE PER QUESTION
03	DISPLAYED STUDENT CUMULATIVE SCORE
04	DISPLAYED STUDENT CUMULATIVE SCORE IN PERCENT
05	DISPLAYED WEIGHT AND ANSWER PER QUESTION
06	DISPLAYED STUDENT ID BY NAME
07	DISPLAYED MINIMAL STUDENT
08	DISPLAYED RESPONSE DISTRIBUTION-REMOTE
09	SELF-CONTAINED PROGRAMMING CAPABILITY
10	CONFIDENTIAL RESPONSE
11	COMPUTER COMPATIBLE-PUNCHED CARD
12	COMPUTER COMPATIBLE-PUNCHED TAPE
13	COMPUTER COMPATIBLE-MAGNETIC TAPE
14	COMPUTER COMPATIBLE-ELECTRICAL INTERFACE
15	AUTOMATED OPERATION-AUDIO/VISUAL
16	AUTOMATED OPERATION-QUESTION AND ANSWER
17	
18	STUDENT REINFORCEMENT CAPABILITY
19	RECORDS RIGHT ANSWER INDICATION
20	RECORDS SPECIFIC WRONG ANSWER
21	RECORDS NO ANSWER INDICATION
22	RECORDS RAW SCORE PER QUESTION
23	RECORDS STUDENT ID BY NUMBER
24	RECORDS STUDENT TOTAL RAW SCORE
25	RECORDS STUDENT PERCENT SCORE
26	RECORDS STUDENT ID BY NAME
27	RESPONSE FREEZE-AUTOMATED
28	RESPONSE FREEZE-MANUAL
29	RESPONSE FREEZE-TIMER
30	STUDENT LOAD UP TO 240
31	STUDENT LOAD UP TO 150
32	STUDENT LOAD UP TO 100
33	STUDENT LOAD UP TO 50
34	STUDENT LOAD UP TO 50
35	STUDENT LOAD UP TO 30
36	STUDENT LOAD UP TO 15
37	STUDENT LOAD UP TO 10
38	MANUAL MEDIA CONTROL
39	RESPONSE-MULTIPLE CHOICE
40	RESPONSE-CONSTRUCTED WRITTEN
41	RESPONSE-CONSTRUCTED SPOKEN
42	RESPONSE-DEMONSTRATED
43	RESPONSE WEIGHTING
44	SINGLE STUDENT USE
45	MODULAR SYSTEM USE
46	RIGHT ANSWER GIVES ELECTRICAL CLOSURE SIGNAL

MACHINE NO CHARACTERISTICS

Machine numbers: 001, 002, 003, 004, 005, 006, 007, 008, 009, 010, 011, 012, 013, 014, 015, 016, 017, 018, 019, 020

P/C

XXXXXXXXAUXXXBIXXX D

INSTRUCTIONAL DEVICE MASTER LIST

DATA GROUP 18c DEVICE CATEGORY   RESPONDERS

(continued)

MACHINE NO   CHARACTERISTICS   P/C

```
              0000000001111111111222222222233333333334444444444555555555 6
              1234567890123456789012345678901234567890123456789012345678 90

021
022
023
024
025
026           1            1    1111 111                    1 1   1        x x x
027                                                         1 1 1 1
028                                                           1 1 1
029                                                         1 1 1 1
```

Overhead Transparency Projectors

NUMBER	MODEL	MANUFACTURER
001	3550 Standard	American Optical Corp.
002	3669/3650 Apollo	American Optical Corp.
003	301 Specialist	Bell and Howell Co.
004	360 Specialist	Bell and Howell Co.
005	15700DYST PortaScribe	Charles Beseler Co.
006	PortaScribe 15710DYST-CC	Charles Beseler Co.
007	PortaScribe Wide 17628-AA	Charles Beseler Co.
008	PortaScribe Wide 17628-SS	Charles Beseler Co.
009	PortaScribe Wide Wide 17627-SS	Charles Beseler Co.
010	7750TH VuGraph	Charles Beseler Co.
011	VuGraph Century VGC614	Charles Beseler Co.
012	6600 Master VuGraph	Charles Beseler Co.
013	80/14	Buhl Optical Co.
014	60014	Buhl Optical Co.
015	ENTRY DELETED*	
016	485 AV	GAF Corp.
017	ENTRY DELETED	
018	Elmo HP-250, 2930	Honeywell, Inc. Photographic Products Division
019	CP-2 Multi-Media Proj.	Hoppmann Corp.
020	Professional, Series 85	Hoppmann Corp.
021	521	3M Company
022	5-088 Desk Top	3M Company
023	567 Glare Free	3M Company
024	Resolute 21105	Projection Optics Co.

*The reader will observe several "Entry Deleted" notations. This is due to last-minute withdrawal of products from the market by manufacturers, and related circumstances.

025	Transpaque Auto-level 20400	Projection Optics Co.
026	Transpaque 20/20 21401	Projection Optics Co.
027	TMC Carri-Vue	T.M. Visual Industries, Inc.
028	Tecnifax 10 inches x 10 inches	Scott Education Division
029	2200 B	Wilson Corp.
030	Executive 2200E	Wilson Corp.
031	PortaScribe G-100	Charles Beseler Co.
032	Specialist 362	Bell and Howell Co.
033	526	3M Company
034	522	3M Company
035	567RGM	3M Company
036	566RGF	3M Company
037	Apollo II Duo-Mag	American Optical Corp.

Audio Tape Recorders/Players

NUMBER	MODEL	MANUFACTURER
001	AX 300	Ampex Corp.
002	Ar-tik 414	Arion Corp.
003	ATC-110A	Audiotronics Corp.
004	ATC-110L	Audiotronics Corp.
005	202A	Electronic Futures, Inc.
006	TP-88	M.P. Audio Corp.
007	AVTM-73	Newcomb Audio Products Co.
008	EDTM-73	Newcomb Audio Products Co.
009	A77	Revox Corp.
010	70TC	Rheem Califone
011	74TC	Rheem Califone
012	RD-708	Sharp Electronics Corp.
013	106 AV	Sony/Superscope, Inc.
014	ENTRY DELETED	
015	7T-20	Teaching Technology Corp.
016	230	Telex Communications Div.
017	RP9511	Visual Educom, Inc.
018	742AV	VM Corp.
019	TR16	White Electronic Development Corp. Ltd.
020	6020AV	Wollensak/3M Co.
021	6200	Wollensak/3M Co.
022	Acousti-Player 700	Acoustifone Corp.
023	Acousti-Corder 700	Acoustifone Corp.
024	Micro 9	Ampex Corp.
025	Micro 14	Ampex Corp.

026	360	Audion Div. of Columbia Scientific Industries, Inc.
027	ATC-130L	Audiotronics Corp.
028	ENTRY DELETED	
029	406	Bell and Howell
030	Casset Tutor 414	Educational Technology, Inc.
031	14-20 Carry Corder	North American Philips Corp.
032	AV80	Rheem Califone
033	CR-5	Rheem Califone
034	RD-403	Sharp Electronics Corp.
035	180-AV	Sony/Superscope, Inc.
036	650	Standard Projector and Equipment Co., Inc.
037	CP-2	Viewlex, Inc.
038	CR-6	Viewlex, Inc.
039	709AV	VM Corp.
040	762AV	VM Corp.
041	ENTRY DELETED	
042	2510AV	Wollensak/3M Co.
043	2530AV	Wollensak/3M Co.
044	2540AV Remote Control	Wollensak/3M Co.
045	4300	Wollensak/3M Co.
046	310	Audion Div. of Columbia Scientific Industries
047	204	Electronic Futures, Inc.
048	APR-20	Mackenzie Laboratories
049	RTD 350	Del Mar Industries
050	Micro 70	Ampex Corp.
051	Repeat-Corder L	Canon USA, Inc.
052	145	Audiotronics Corp.

053	GX-365	Akai of America
054	GX-365D	Akai of America
055	X330	Akai of America
056	CS-50	Akai of America
057	CS-50D	Akai of America
058	CR-80	Akai of America
059	CR-80D	Akai of America
060	20/50	Avid Corp.
061	6000 X Deck	Tandberg of America
062	3000 X Deck	Tandberg of America
063	4000 X	Tandberg of America
064	Series 14	Tandberg of America
065	Series 15 F	Tandberg of America
066	Series 15SL	Tandberg of America
067	Series 11	Tandberg of America
068	Cassette Audio-Comparator	Telex Communications Division
069	Cassette Recorder-Player	Telex Communications Division
070	Cassette Player	Telex Communications Division
071	CR-8	Viewlex, Inc.
072	742AV	VM Corp.
073	780AV	VM Corp.
074	707	VM Corp.
075	405	Bell and Howell Co.
076	3050 and 3060	Bell and Howell Co.
077	2392	Bell and Howell Co.
078	3040	Bell and Howell Co.
079	RD418	Sharp Electronics Corp.
080	RD 429U	Sharp Electronics Corp.

081	ENTRY DELETED	
082	RD709	Sharp Electronics Corp.
083	ENTRY DELETED	
084	ENTRY DELETED	
085	ENTRY DELETED	
086	ENTRY DELETED	
087	ENTRY DELETED	
088	ENTRY DELETED	
089	Audio Communicator	Educational Sound Systems
090	LCH1000	North American Philips Corp.

Slide Projectors

NUMBER	MODEL	MANUFACTURER
001	Bauer S1 Autofocus	Allied Impex Corp.
002	1200 Carousel	A.V.E. Corp.
003	Bergen-Atlantic 450	Bergen Expo Systems, Inc.
004	Lightning-600	Bergen Expo Systems, Inc.
005	O-R-1000	Bergen Expo Systems, Inc.
006	1406-144 Fleetwood	Brumberger Co., Inc.
007	1422-144 Riviera	Brumberger Co., Inc.
008	Hi-Lite 820-800	Buhl Optical Co.
009	Cine-Slide 325	Busch Film and Equipment Co.
010	ENTRY DELETED	
011	Carobeam	Decision Systems, Inc.
012	Kodak Ektagraphic AF-2	Eastman Kodak Co.
013	Kodak Ektagraphic ARC	Eastman Kodak Co.
014	Kodak Ektagraphic B-2	Eastman Kodak Co.
015	Kodak Ektagraphic E-2	Eastman Kodak Co.
016	Mor-Lite	Fortune Audio Visual
017	970 A/V	GAF Corp.
018	Executive	Graflex Division, Singer Co.
019	Traveler	Graflex Division, Singer Co.
020	ENTRY DELETED	
021	Preview, AVII, 6694	Honeywell Inc., Photographic Products Division
022	P-2	Hoppmann Corp.
023	Prima HP1 No. 345	Hudson Photographic Ind., Inc.
024	Caralite Mark 3	International Audio Visual, Inc.
025	RPT-500 Rear Projection Theaterama One System	Motiva, Ltd.

026	71 Highlight	Presentation Tech. Aids, Inc.
027	Super Light 3402	Realist, Inc.
028	ENTRY DELETED	
029	Selectroslide SLR-1200A	Spindler and Sauppe, Inc.
030	Dual Selectroslide SLD-1200A	Spindler and Sauppe, Inc.
031	ENTRY DELETED	
032	12	Tel-A-Story, Inc.
033	TMC Showmatic 2007S	T.M. Visual Industries, Inc.
034	Perkeo Automat S250	Zeiss Ikon
035	Sound Cine-Slide 325 SS	Busch Film and Equipment Co.
036	CV-411	Colorado Visual Aids Supply Co.
037	Coxco Sound/Slide SP120	Cox Communications, Inc.
038	Cinema Sound 750	Creatron, Inc.
039	Cinema Sound 1650	Creatron, Inc.
040	Sonomatic RP	Harwald Co.
041	Teleshow I NP-34SRP	Hoppmann Corp.
042	Teleshow II H34-S	Hoppmann Corp.
043	Kalavox, Model 392 plus Kodak Carousel Proj.	Kalart Victor Corp.
044	525 Sound-On-Slide System	3M Co., Visual Products Division
045	ENTRY DELETED	
046	ENTRY DELETED	
047	Robot RA-110	Programo, Inc.
048	Synchromedia	Setco Audio-Visual, Inc.
049	TMC Synchromatic AV 2000	T.M. Visual Industries, Inc.
050	TD201	Teaching Dynamics, Inc.
051	981Q2 Slide Cube	Bell and Howell Co.

052	Atlantic 1000	Bergen Expo Systems, Inc.
053	BFL 450-46	Christie Electric Corp.
054	Rotoshow 150-000	GAF Corp.

Filmstrip Projectors

NUMBER	MODEL	MANUFACTURER
001	745-C Specialist	Bell and Howell Co., Audio Visual Division
002	28A6A	Dukane Corp.
003	ENTRY DELETED	
004	SM-1000RC	Graflex Division, Singer
005	School Master 500 Remote	Graflex Division, Singer
006	School Master 750 Remote	Graflex Division, Singer
007	Prima HPI NNo. 340	Hudson Photographic Industries, Inc.
008	Victor-Soundview PhD	Kalart Victor Corp.
009	Victor-Soundview PS-65	Kalart Victor Corp.
010	666C	Standard Projector and Equipment Co., Inc.
011	333-RC	Standard Projector and Equipment Co., Inc.
012	444 Dual	Standard Projector and Equipment Co., Inc.
013	500-CZ	Standard Projector and Equipment Co., Inc.
014	500 FS	Standard Projector and Equipment Co., Inc.
015	500-RR	Standard Projector and Equipment Co., Inc.
016	750-AB	Standard Projector and Equipment Co., Inc.
017	750-C	Standard Projector and Equipment Co., Inc.
018	1000-C	Standard Projector and Equipment Co., Inc.
019	TMC Showoff 2010	T.M. Visual Industries, Inc.
020	Model B	Viewlex, Inc.
021	V-1 Mini-Giant	Viewlex, Inc.
022	V-8	Viewlex, Inc.
023	V-8R	Viewlex, Inc.
024	V-25	Viewlex, Inc.
025	V-25R	Viewlex, Inc.

026	V-45	Viewlex, Inc.
027	V-85	Viewlex, Inc.
028	V-500	Viewlex, Inc.
029	V-1200 Magnum	Viewlex, Inc.
030	Braun D7	Braun Electric Canada, Ltd.
031	Study Mate II	Graflex Division, Singer
032	ENTRY DELETED	
033	E-Z Viewer	Graflex Division, Singer
034	Prima HPI No. 330	Hudson Photographic Industries, Inc.
035	201	Standard Projector and Equipment Co., Inc.
036	777	Standard Projector and Equipment Co., Inc.
037	999	Standard Projector and Equipment Co., Inc.
038	1491	Standard Projector and Equipment Co., Inc.
039	1495	Standard Projector and Equipment Co., Inc.
040	1995	Standard Projector and Equipment Co., Inc.
041	Previewer Junior No. 1	Viewlex, Inc.
042	Previewer Senior	Viewlex, Inc.
043	FS-100	Whitehouse Products, Inc.
044	VR-255-159	Viewlex, Inc.
045	150 Watt Filmstrip	Avid Corp.
046	30 Watt Filmstrip	Avid Corp.
047	AV8	Avid Corp.

Sound Filmstrip Projectors

NUMBER	MODEL	MANUFACTURER
001	TSM	Audiscan, Inc.
002	1151-B Attache 35	Bell and Howell Co.
003	505/33000	Charles Beseler Co.
004	Salesmate 8500 MII	Charles Beseler Co.
005	14A285F	Dukane Corp.
006	14A335F	Dukane Corp.
007	14A395C	Dukane Corp.
008	14A500E	Dukane Corp.
009	14A543D	Dukane Corp.
010	14A650B	Dukane Corp.
011	28A11A	Dukane Corp.
012	28A14 Cassette Commander	Dukane Corp.
013	28A15A Micromatic	Dukane Corp.
014	28A25	Dukane Corp.
015	A-1000	General Learning Corp., Media Division
016	Audio-Master Executive	H-R Productions, Inc.
017	Audio-Master Special I	H-R Productions, Inc.
018	Victor-Soundview SAT-65D	Kalart Victor Corp.
019	Courier I	LaBelle Industries, Inc.
020	Courier 16	LaBelle Industries, Inc.
021	Sentinel 16	LaBelle Industries, Inc.
022	Sentinel 35	LaBelle Industries, Inc.
023	Tutor 16	LaBelle Industries, Inc.
024	400FC	McClure Projectors, Inc.
025	CSA-A/50	McClure Projectors, Inc.

026	CSM-P Cassette-Strip	McClure Projectors, Inc.
027	Picturephone 400	McClure Projectors, Inc.
028	Mastermatic II35MM	Optisonics Corp.
029	RCS MODule System Model Ms10 AV Set	Retention Communication Systems, Inc.
030	ENTRY DELETED	
031	40, Combination 1	Standard Projector and Equipment Co., Inc.
032	Combination 50/750 AB	Standard Projector and Equipment Co., Inc.
033	60, Combination 11	Standard Projector and Equipment Co., Inc.
034	60A, Combination 17	Standard Projector and Equipment Co., Inc.
035	600, Combination 31	Standard Projector and Equipment Co., Inc.
036	Showoff/Soundoff 865	T.M. Visual Industries, Inc.
037	Showtalk V-8R	Viewlex, Inc.
038	Showtalk Cassette Series V-8R	Viewlex, Inc.
039	SSA Sight n Sound Teaching Station	Viewlex, Inc.
040	SSAC Sight n Sound Teaching Station	Viewlex, Inc.
041	Viewtalk VHA Series	Viewlex, Inc.
042	Viewtalk Cassette Series VHAC 3	Viewlex, Inc.
043	Viewtalk VTA-22 R	Viewlex, Inc.
044	FS-250	Whitehouse Products, Inc.
045	Audio Study Mate	Graflex Division, Singer Co.
046	V-136	Viewlex, Inc.
047	V-192	Viewlex, Inc.
048	Auto Vance II Study Mate	Graflex Division, Singer
049	Messenger VII	Graflex Division, Singer
050	Audiscan 2000	Audiscan, Inc.

051	Audiscan 3000	Audiscan, Inc.
052	Response A-V Matic 28A29	Dukane Corp.
053	Super Micromatic 28A28	Dukane Corp.
054	AV-8 and AV-550	Avid Corp.
055	V135 Sight/Sound	Viewlex, Inc.
056	V191	Viewlex, Inc.
057	TE2020 (PIP)	North American Philips Corp.

16mm Projectors

NUMBER	MODEL	MANUFACTURER
001	Bauer P6 Automatic Model M152	Allied Impex Corp.
002	Bauer P6 Automatic 300 Model L	Allied Impex Corp.
003	Bauer Selection 11-0 Type SL3/1600	Allied Impex Corp.
004	Bauer Selection Studio Single System	Allied Impex Corp.
005	Canary	A.V.E. Corp.
006	Professional X-300 Xenon	A.V.E. Corp.
007	X-300	A.V.E. Corp.
008	614 CE Commercial JAN	Bell and Howell Co.
009	8302L	Bell and Howell Co.
010	566T Specialist Autoload Filmosound	Bell and Howell Co.
011	1552 Specialist Autoload Filmosound	Bell and Howell Co.
012	O-R-1000	Bergen Expo Systems, Inc.
013	XE-600	Bergen Expo Systems, Inc.
014	Cine-Educator 6240 MP	Busch Film and Equipment Co.
015	Cinesalesman 3	Busch Film and Equipment Co.
016	Cinesalesman 4A	Busch Film and Equipment Co.
017	Two-Way 6A	Busch Film and Equipment Co.
018	BFN900-51E, Xenolite	Christie Electric Corp. Xenolite Division
019	BFN900-256E, Xenolite	Christie Electric Corp. Xenolite Division
020	BFP900-614E, Xenolite	Christie Electric Corp. Xenolite Division
021	Kodak Pageant Arc	Eastman Kodak Co.

022	Kodak Pageant Sound AV-12E6	Eastman Kodak Co.
023	Kodak Pageant Sound AV-105-M	Eastman Kodak Co.
024	Kodak Pageant Sound AV-126-TR	Eastman Kodak Co.
025	ENTRY DELETED	
026	Model 920R	Graflex Division, Singer
027	Model 1015	Graflex Division, Singer
028	Model 1040	Graflex Division, Singer
029	Model 1050	Graflex Division, Singer
030	Insta-Load Model 11 20	Graflex Division, Singer
031	Cinematic	Harwald Co.
032	Elmo Self-threading 16MM Filmatic 16-SS	Honeywell Inc., Photographic Products Division
033	Elmo FS16-1000S	Honeywell Inc., Photographic Products Division
034	DaMaster Mark IV	Hoover Brothers, Inc.
035	Teleshow I-NP34M	Hoppmann Corp.
036	Premier EX1510	International Audio Visual, Inc.
037	Royal M-O	International Audio Visual, Inc.
038	Royal M-3	International Audio Visual, Inc.
039	Royal ST-OH	International Audio Visual, Inc.
040	Royal ST-OH-CAK	International Audio Visual, Inc.
041	Royal ST-3H	International Audio Visual, Inc.
042	Supreme EX-5000	International Audio Visual, Inc.
043	Duolite ST-18	Kalart Victor Corp.
044	Modular Moviematic Mark IV	Kalart Victor Corp.
045	Movie STM-3C Custom	Kalart Victor Corp.
046	Moviematic STM-18	Kalart Victor Corp.
047	70-15	Kalart Victor Corp.

048	70-25	Kalart Victor Corp.
049	75-15	Kalart Victor Corp.
050	75-15 MC3	Kalart Victor Corp.
051	75-25	Kalart Victor Corp.
052	82-25 MPR	Kalart Victor Corp.
053	PJ-16	Magna-Tech Electronic Co., Inc.
054	Bolex S-321	Paillard, Inc.
055	Tel-JANX9-CE	Telepro Industries, Inc.
056	5-1200	Triangle Projectors, Inc.
057	Cinesound 16	Viewlex, Inc.
058	JAN 2	Viewlex, Inc.
059	JAN-5	Viewlex, Inc.
060	ENTRY DELETED	
061	AAP 300V Motion Analyzer	Lafayette Instrument Co.
062	XF450	Bergen Expo Systems, Inc.
063	1540	Bell and Howell Co.
064	1545	Bell and Howell Co.
065	1550	Bell and Howell Co.
066	1040	Graflex Div. of Singer
067	1115	Graflex Div. of Singer
068	1120	Graflex Div. of Singer
069	1160	Graflex Div. of Singer
070	1170	Graflex Div. of Singer
071	70-0	Kalart Victor Corp.
072	256TR	Eastman Kodak Co.
073	AAP700	Lafayette Instrument Co.
074	224A	L and W Photo, Inc.
075	224 M/R	L and W Photo, Inc.

076	Marc 300 JAN 3 MC	Viewlex, Inc.
077	Marc 300 JAN 6 MC	Viewlex, Inc.
078	35043-AT59	Viewlex, Inc.
079	35181-AT59	Viewlex, Inc.
080	R35044-T59	Viewlex, Inc.
081	222-A Photo Optical Data Analyzer	L and W Photo, Inc.
082	302L	Bell and Howell Co.
083	900B	L and W Photo, Inc.

8mm Projectors

NUMBER	MODEL	MANUFACTURER
001	Bauer T30	Allied Impex Corp.
002	Institor	Bohn Benton, Inc.
003	Noris Norimat	Braun Electric Canada, Ltd.
004	Model 60	Dick, A.B. Co.
005	28A8	Dukane Corp.
006	Kodak Ektagraphic MFS-8	Eastman Kodak Co.
007	Ektagraphic Sound 8	Eastman Kodak Co.
008	Ektagraphic 120 Movie	Eastman Kodak Co.
009	Instamatic M100A	Eastman Kodak Co.
010	Mark S-709	Eumig (USA), Inc.
011	Mark-S-712	Eumig (USA), Inc.
012	ENTRY DELETED	
013	711	Fairchild Camera and Instrument Corp.
014	Seventy-21	Fairchild Camera and Instrument Corp.
015	Seventy-31	Fairchild Camera and Instrument Corp.
016	Seventy-41	Fairchild Camera and Instrument Corp.
017	1788Z	GAF Corp.
018	Norimat S	Karl Heitz, Inc.
019	Heurtier Dual S-8	Hervic Corp./Cinema Beaulieu
020	Heurtier Dual Super 8 with Sound Module	Hervic Corp./Cinema Beaulieu
021	Elmo ST8MO	Honeywell Inc., Photographic Products Division
022	2MS	Jayark Instruments Corp.
023	Instant-View 510A	McClure Projectors, Inc.
024	Super 8 Sound Motion Picture	MPO Videotronic Projector Corp.

025	Norelco PIP Audio-Visual Cassette System (Model TE 2020)	North American Philips Corp.
026	Bolex SM-8	Paillard, Inc.
027	Bolex 18-5	Paillard, Inc.
028	SP169	Synchronex Corp.
029	SP-500	Synchronex Corp.
030	SRP-500	Synchronex Corp.
031	ENTRY DELETED	
032	610 Movie-Vision Console	Technicolor, Inc., Commercial and Educational Division
033	ENTRY DELETED	
034	1000B	Technicolor, Inc., Commercial and Educational Division
035	1300	Technicolor, Inc., Commercial and Educational Division
036	V-193	Viewlex, Inc.
037	ENTRY DELETED	
038	86AZR	DeJur Amsco Corp.
039	AAP-900V	Lafayette Instrument Co.
040	1400	Technicolor, Inc., Commercial and Educational Division
041	820	Technicolor, Inc., Commercial and Educational Division
042	520	Technicolor, Inc., Commercial and Educational Division
043	346	Bell and Howell Co.
044	357	Bell and Howell Co.
045	ENTRY DELETED	
046	456	Bell and Howell Co.
047	ENTRY DELETED	
048	458SZ	Bell and Howell Co.

049	468SZ	Bell and Howell Co.
050	Eumig Mark S 51OD	W. Carsen Co. Ltd.
051	Eumig Mark S 711R	W. Carsen Co. Ltd.
052	Seventy-07	Fairchild Camera and Instrument Corp.
053	Console Model Videotronic Super 8	MPO Videotronic Projector Corp.
054	Exhibit Model Videotronic Super 8	MPO Videotronic Projector Corp.
055	Bolex 18-9 DVO	Paillard, Inc.
056	Bolex Multimatic (Silent)	Paillard, Inc. Paillard, Inc.
057	V-190	Viewlex, Inc.
058	V-192	Viewlex, Inc.

Microform Devices

NUMBER	MODEL	MANUFACTURER
001	PMR/50	DASA Corporation
002	COM 1	Dioptrix, Inc.
003	27A5	Dukane Corp.
004	ENTRY DELETED	
005	Exp 14	Dukane Corp.
006	Standard	Realist, Inc.
007	Vista	Realist, Inc.
008	Vantage	Realist, Inc.
009	Book Size Module	Microdisplays Systems, Inc.
010	300	T.M. Visual Industries, Inc.
011	Robot L-36	Karl Heitz, Inc.
012	22/40	University Microfilms
013	14/14	University Microfilms
014	Motor Matic	Eastman Kodak Co.
015	Easa-Matic	Eastman Kodak Co.
016	Micro Star	Eastman Kodak Co.
017	P.V.M.	Eastman Kodak Co.
018	Mira Code	Eastman Kodak Co.
019	576-90	Dukane Corp.
020	9/12-I	University Microfilms
021	9/12-II	University Microfilms
022	201	Image Systems, Inc.
023	400	Taylor Merchant Corp.
024	Hand Viewer	Taylor Merchant Corp.
025	Morgan 200	Morgan Information Systems, Inc.
026	Morgan 100	Morgan Information Systems, Inc.
027	95	Micrographic Technology Corp.

Teaching Machines

NUMBER	MODEL	MANUFACTURER
001	APT A/V Tutor	Gemco, Inc.
002	Telor	Enrich Corp.
003	Autotutor	Sargent-Welch Scientific Co.
004	Mast Learning System Model 1700	Mast Development Co.
005	ENTRY DELETED	
006	Dorsett M-86	Dorsett Educational Systems, Inc.
007	System 80	Borg-Warner Educational Systems
008	AVS-10	CBS Labs/Viewlex
009	ENTRY DELETED	
010	ENTRY DELETED	
011	I -250	Singer Co., Simulation Products Div.
012	Coxco RB305	Cox Communications, Inc.
013	Self Development Computer	Self Development, Inc.
014	Avidesk	Avid Corp.
015	Min/Max	R.H. Hintley Co.
016	Responder with Sound-O-Matic III	Optisonics Corp.
017	The Didactor	Didactics Corp.
018	Speed Model 2000	McMahon Electronic Engineering
019	Speed Model 2100	McMahon Electronic Engineering
020	Mark III 520	Hu-Mac, Inc.
021	Audio Vision MK-10	Ken Cook Transnational
022	C.A.I.	Hypertech Corp.
023	Series 70	Hoppmann Corp.
024	Test Mate Responder with A/V Unit	Instructive Devices, Inc.
025	MARK 9	Ken Cook Transnational
026	MARK 7	Ken Cook Transnational

Video Tape Recorders and Players

NUMBER	MODEL	MANUFACTURER
001	VP-4500	Ampex Corp.
002	VPR-5200	Ampex Corp.
003	VPR-5800	Ampex Corp.
004	VPR-7900	Ampex Corp.
005	VR-5100	Ampex Corp.
006	PVR-707	Audiotronics Corp. Video Systems Division
007	VTR-820	Concord Electronics Corp.
008	VTR-1000	Concord Electronics Corp.
009	VTR-3000	Concord Electronics Corp.
010	DP-2	Diamond Power Electronics
011	DP-3	Diamond Power Electronics
012	4TD1B1	GBC Closed Circuit TV Corp.
013	X400	Javelin Electronics Corp.
014	700	JFD Systems, Div. of Riker Commun.
015	SV-510	Shibaden Corp. of America
016	SV-700UC	Shibaden Corp. of America
017	ENTRY DELETED	
018	ENTRY DELETED	
019	EV-320 F	Sony Corp. of America
020	EVR Teleplayer	Motorola Systems, Inc.
021	700PB	IVC-International Video Corp.
022	700	IVC-International Video Corp.
023	760	IVC-International Video Corp.
024	800A	IVC-International Video Corp.
025	820	IVC-International Video Corp.

026	870C	IVC-International Video Corp.
027	900-C	IVC-International Video Corp.
028	AV3600	Sony Corp of America
029	AV3650	Sony Corp of America
030	VP1000	Sony Corp of America
031	VO1600	Sony Corp of America
032	VT700	Akai Corp of America

Portable Video Tape Recording Systems

NUMBER	MODEL	MANUFACTURER
001	VTR-450T	Concord Electronics Corp.
002	LDL-1000	North American Philips Broadcasting Equipment Corp.
003	SV-707U.FP-707	Shibaden Corp. of America
004	VTS-110DX	Akai Corp. of America
005	INSTAVIDEO	Ampex Corp.
006	AV-3400/AVC-3400	Sony Corp. of America
007	NV-3080/WV-8080	Panasonic Corp.
008	VT-100	Akai Corp. of America

TV Monitors and Projectors

NUMBER	MODEL	MANUFACTURER
001	12VM205	Javelin Electronics Corp.
002	TM9	Javelin Electronics Corp.
003	TM16	Javelin Electronics Corp.
004	TM23	Javelin Electronics Corp.
005	T-980	Magnavox Co.
006	T-5916	Magnavox Co.
007	T-5905	Magnavox Co.
008	5M916RM3	Setchell Carlson Co.
009	6M912	Setchell Carlson Co.
010	9M912	Setchell Carlson Co.
011	3M912S	Setchell Carlson Co.
012	9M912R	Setchell Carlson Co.
013	3ER2100	Setchell Carlson Co.
014	5EC904	Setchell Carlson Co.
015	10M915RL	Setchell Carlson Co.
016	10M915RT	Setchell Carlson Co.
017	9MC914	Setchell Carlson Co.
018	9MC914R	Setchell Carlson Co.
019	5MC914	Setchell Carlson Co.
020	MMA16	Audiotronics Corp.
021	MMA19	Audiotronics Corp.
022	MMA10	Audiotronics Corp.
023	MMR23	Audiotronics Corp.
024	AN-69V	Panasonic
025	TR-413V	Panasonic
026	TN-932	Panasonic

027	TN-952	Panasonic
028	CT-25V	Panasonic
029	AN-236V	Panasonic
030	TR-910M	Panasonic
031	TR-910V	Panasonic
032	200A	Amphicon Systems, Inc.
033	270	Amphicon Systems, Inc.
034	1000E	Amphicon Systems, Inc.
035	VP-1	GBC Closed Circuit TV Corp.
036	Tele-Beam A912 ACP	Kalart Victor Corp.
037	PJ700	General Electric Co.
038	PJ500	General Electric Co.
039	260A	Amphicon Systems, Inc.

Audio-Visual Integrators

NUMBER	MODEL	MANUFACTURER
001	AVS-700	Audio Visual Systems, Inc.
002	Coxco/Municator Series Y	Cox Communications, Inc.
003	SR-3	General Techniques, Inc.
004	Cue Slide	Klitten Co., Inc.
005	Pla-Matic 83	LaBelle Industries, Inc.
006	ENTRY DELETED	
007	Norelco Synchroplayer (TE821)	North American Philips Corp.
008	Norelco Synchrotutor (TE822)	North American Philips Corp.
009	Sound-O-Matic III	Optisonics Corp.
010	Caro Vox CVP 100	Programo, Inc.
011	SSP-1	Saunders Associates, Inc.
012	SUBM-2	Saunders Associates, Inc.
013	TR-1 Pacer	Saunders Associates, Inc.
014	ENTRY DELETED	
015	Tri-Tone I	Mackenzie Laboratories
016	Super Sync	Instructomatic, Inc.
017	Audio Mate 600	Montage Productions, Inc.
018	Narrator 1000	Montage Productions, Inc.
019	TD 301	Teaching Dynamics, Inc.
020	Audio Link IV	Link Educational Laboratories
021	V.M. 703 AV	VM Corp.
022	System 240C	Saunders Associates, Inc.
023	505 with Slide Synch.	Avid Corporation
024	AVS 600	Audio Visual Systems, Inc.

025	Audion 360	Audion Division of Columbia Scientific Industries
026	28A18 Recorder/Pulser	Dukane Corp.
027	Synchro-Recorder	Orrtronics Products
028	Synchro-Repeater	Orrtronics Products
029	Programmer	Avid Corporation
030	350	Audion Division of Columbia Scientific Industries
031	30	Audion Division of Columbia Scientific Industries
032	31 and 85 System	Audion Division of Columbia Scientific Industries
033	2550	Wollensak/3M Co.
034	Tape/Slide Synchronizer 2	Tandberg of America
035	LCH 1000PR	North American Philips Corp.
036	752 AV	VM Corp.
037	756 AV	VM Corp.

Random Access Devices

NUMBER	MODEL	MANUFACTURER
001	BFL450-46Xenolite with Kodak Ektagraphic	Christie Electric Corp., Xenolite Div.
002	DSI Model 80 RA	Decision Systems, Inc.
003	Kodak Ektagraphic RA-960	Eastman Kodak Co.
004	970 AV plus Slide Seeker	GAF Corp.
005	RA80 Random Access Module and Carousel Proj.	Hoppmann Corporation
006	138-6 Multiple Control System	Mast Development Co.
007	ENTRY DELETED	
008	Selectroslide SLS-750B	Spindler and Sauppe, Inc.
009	Selectroslide SLX-750B	Spindler and Sauppe, Inc.
010	RA-100	Telepro Industries, Inc.
011	RA-500	Telepro Industries, Inc.
012	GAF 1000	GAF Corporation
013	Carobeam B	Decision Systems, Inc.
014	Mor Lite R.A.	Fortune Audio Visual
015	132B	Mast Development Co.
016	137-H	Mast Development Co.
017	Mast/Kalavox Random Access A.V. Projector	Kalart Victor and Mast Development Co.

Responders

NUMBER	MODEL	MANUFACTURER
001	Educom Validator	Visual Educom, Inc.
002	Edex 300 Series Communicator	Visual Educom, Inc.
003	Edex Media Master Series 650A	Visual Educom, Inc.
004	AIDS	Visual Educom, Inc.
005	RESYC 600	Response Systems Corp.
006	R-E-S	Charles Beseler Co.
007	Mata Response System	Scott Education Division
008	Responadex	T.M. Visual Industries, Inc.
009	QRS 681-F	Quick Response Systems, Inc.
010	QRS 681-RCP	Quick Response Systems, Inc.
011	QRS 681-MS	Quick Response Systems, Inc.
012	Student Response Monitor	Gemco, Inc.
013	ASRM	Gemco, Inc.
014	Test Mate Responder (Mod II)	Instructive Devices, Inc.
015	Test Mate Responder (Mod I)	Instructive Devices, Inc.
016	L-3000	Singer Co.
017	L-2000	Singer Co.
018	Model 703-1	Carmody Corp.
019	ENTRY DELETED	
020	RB- 30S	Cox Communications, Inc.
021	ENTRY DELETED	
022	ENTRY DELETED	
023	ENTRY DELETED	
024	ENTRY DELETED	

025	ENTRY DELETED	
026	Answer Cube	Produce locally
027	Written Test	Produce locally
028	Oral Test	Produce locally
029	Practical Test	Produce locally

List of Manufacturers

List of Manufacturers

Acoustifone Corp.
20149 Sunburst Street
Chatsworth, California 91311

Akai Corp. of America Ltd.
2139 East Deltmo Boulevard
Compton, California 90224

Allied Impex Corp.
c/o Interstate Photo Supply Corp.
168 Glen Cove Road
Carle Place, New York 11514

American Optical Corp.
Eggert Road
Buffalo, New York 14226

Ampex Corp.
2201 Estes Avenue
Elk Grove Village, Illinois 60007

Amphicon Systems, Inc.
1 Graphic Place
Moonachie, New Jersey 07074

Arion Corp.
825 Boone Avenue, North
Minneapolis, Minnesota 55427

Audion Div. of
Columbia Scientific Industries, Inc.
P.O. Box 6190
3625 Ed Bluestein Boulevard
Austin, Texas 78702

Audiotronics Corp.
Video Systems Div.
P.O. Box 151
7428 Bellaire Avenue
North Hollywood, California 91603

Audio Visual Systems, Inc.
1219 East 4th Avenue
Denver, Colorado 80218

Audiscan, Inc.
P.O. Box 1456
Bellevue, Washington 98005

A.V.E. Corp.
250 West 54th Street
New York, New York 10019

Avid Corp.
P M and E Electronics Division
10 Tripps Lane
East Providence, Rhode Island 02914

Bell and Howell Co.
Audio Visual Division
7100 McCormick Road
Chicago, Illlnois 60645

Bergen Expo Systems, Inc.
Route 46
Lodi, New Jersey 07644

Beseler, Charles Co.
219 South 18th Street
East Orange, New Jersey 07018

Bohn Benton
110 Roosevelt Avenue
Mineola, New York 11501

Borg-Warner
Educational Systems
7450 North Natcheg Avenue
Niles, Illinois 60648

Braun Electric Canada, Ltd.
3269 American Drive
Malton, Ontario, Canada

Brumberger Co., Inc.
1948 Troutman Street
Brooklyn, New York 11237

Buhl Optical Co.
1776 New Highway
Farmingdale, New York 11735

Busch Film and Equipment Co.
214 South Hamilton
Saginaw, Michigan 48602

Canon USA, Inc.
10 Nevada Drive
Lake Success, New York 11040

Carmody Corp.
2361 Wehrle Drive
Buffalo, New York 14221

Carsen, W. Co. Ltd.
Eumig
31 Scarsdale Road
Don Mills, Toronto, Ontario

CBS Labs/Viewlex
Holbrook, New York 11741

Christie Electric Corp.
3410 West 67th Street
Los Angeles, California 90805

Colorado Visual Aids Supply Co.
955 Bannock Street
Denver, Colorado 80204

Concord Electronics Corp.
1935 Armacost Avenue
Los Angeles, California 90025

Cook, Ken Transnational Co.
9929 West Silver Spring Road
Milwaukee, Wisconsin 53225

Cox Communications, Inc.
915 Howard Street
San Francisco, California 94103

Creatron, Inc.
36 Cherry Lane
Floral Park, New York 11001

DASA Corporation
15 Stevens Street
Andover, Massachusetts 01810

Decision Systems, Inc.
East 66 Midland Avenue
Paramus, New Jersey 07625

DeJur Amsco Corp.
45-01 Northern Boulevard
Long Island City, New York 11101

Del Mar Industries
10457 Roselle
San Diego, California 92121

Deltek Business Machines
Division of Dodwell and Co., Ltd.
120 Wall Street
New York, New York 10005

Diamond Power Electronics
Box 415
Lancaster, Ohio 43130

Dick, A.B. Co.
5700 West Touhy Avenue
Niles, Illinois 60648

Didactics Corp.
700 Grace Street
Mansfield, Ohio 44905

Dioptrix, Inc.
1020 Prospect Street
La Jolla, California 92037

Dorsett Educational
Systems, Inc.
P.O. Box 1226
1225 West Main Street
Norman, Oklahoma 73069

Dukane Corp.
103 North 11th Avenue
Saint Charles, Illinois 60174

Eastman Kodak Co.
343 State Street
Rochester, New York 14650

Educational Sound
Systems, Inc.
540 East New Haven Avenue
Melbourne, Florida 32901

Educational Technology, Inc.
2224 Hewlett Avenue
Merrick, New York 11566

Electronic Futures, Inc.
Division of KMS Industries, Inc.
57 Dodge Avenue
North Haven, Connecticut 06473

Enrich Corp.
3437 Alma Street
Palo Alto, California 94306

Eumig (USA), Inc.
110 West 31st Street
New York, New York 10001

Fairchild Camera and
Instrument Corp.
75 Mall Drive
Commack, New York 11725

Fortune Audio Visual
35 Bergen Turnpike
Little Ferry, New Jersey 07643

GAF Corp.
140 West 51st Street
New York, New York 10020

GBC Closed Circuit TV Corp.
74 5th Avenue
New York, New York 10011

Gemco, Inc.
7700 East 38th Street
Tulsa, Oklahoma 74145

General Electric Co.
Visual Communication
Product Department
Electronics Park
Syracuse, New York 13201

General Learning Corp.
Media Division
250 James Street
Morristown, New Jersey 07960

General Techniques, Inc.
1270 Broadway
New York, New York 10001

Graflex, Singer Co.
3750 Monroe Avenue
Rochester, New York 14603

Gregory Magnetic Industries, Inc.
317 South West Fifth Street
Pompano Beach, Florida 33060

Harwald Co.
1245 Chicago Avenue
Evanston, Illinois 60202

Heitz, Karl, Inc.
979 Third Avenue
New York, New York 10022

Hervic Corp./Cinema Beaulieu
14225 Ventura Boulevard
Sherman Oaks, California 91403

Hintley Co., R.H.
575 Lexington Avenue
New York, New York 10022

Honeywell, Inc.
Photographic Products Division
5501 Broadway
Littleton, Colorado 80120

Honor Products Co.
20 Moulton Street
Cambridge, Massachusetts 02138

Hoover Brothers, Inc.
1305 North 14th Street
Temple, Texas 76501

Hoppmann Corp.
5410 Port Royal Road
Springfield, Virginia 22150

H-R Productions, Inc.
121 West 45th Street
New York, New York 10036

Hudson Photographic
Industries, Inc.
2 South Buckhout Street
Irvington-on-Hudson, New York 10553

Hu-Mac, Inc.
2415 Chareston Road
Mountain View, California 94040

Hypertech Corp.
7343 West Wilson Avenue
Harwood Heights, Illinois 60656

Image Systems, Inc.
11244 Playa Court
Culver City, California 90230

Instructive Devices, Inc.
147 Armistice Boulevard
Pawtucket, Rhode Island 02860

Instructomatic, Inc.
30625 West Eight Mile Road
Livonia, Michigan 48152

International Audio
Visual, Inc.
119 Blanchard Street
Seattle, Washington 98121

IVC-International Video Corp.
675 Almanor Avenue
Sunnyvale, California 94086

Javelin Electronics Corp.
5556 West Washington Boulevard
Los Angeles, California 90016

Jayark Instruments Corp.
10 East 49th Street
New York, New York 10017

JFD Systems, Division of
Riker Communications
14 Orchard Street
Norwalk, Connecticut 06850

Kalart Victor Corp.
Hultenius Avenue
Plainsville, Connecticut 06062

Klitten Co., Inc.
1213 North Amalfi Drive
Pacific Palisades, California 90272

LaBelle Industries, Inc.
510 South Worthington Street
Oconomoc, Wisconsin 53066

Lafayette Instrument Co.
P.O. Box 1279
Lafayette, Indiana 47902

Link Educational Laboratories
P.O. Box 11073
Montgomery, Alabama 36111

L and W Photo, Inc.
15451 Cabrito Road
Van Nuys, California 91406

Mackenzie Laboratories
P.O. Box 3503
South El Monte, California 91733

Magna-Tech Electronic Co., Inc.
630 Ninth Avenue
New York, New York 10036

Magnavox Co.
1700 Magnavox Way
Fort Wayne, Indiana 46804

Mast Development Co.
2212 East 12th Street
Davenport, Iowa 52802

McClure Projectors, Inc.
P.O. Box 7
1215 Washington Avenue
Wilmette, Illinois 60091

McMahon Electronic
Engineering
381 West 7th Street
San Pedro, California 90731

Microdisplays Systems, Inc.
c/o Retention Communication
Systems, Inc.
2 Pennsylvania Plaza
Suite 1199
New York, New York 10001

Micrographic Technology Corp.
1732 Kaiser Avenue
Santa Ana, California 92702

3M Co.
Visual Products Division
3 North Center
Saint Paul, Minnesota 55101

Montage Productions, Inc.
49 West 27th Street
New York, New York 10001

Morgan Information Systems, Inc.
193 Constitution Drive
Menlo Park, California 94025

Motiva, Ltd.
155 East 55th Street
New York, New York 10022

Motorola Systems, Inc.
4501 W. Augusta Boulevard
Chicago, Illinois 60651

M.P. Audio Corp.
Fairfield, Connecticut 06430

MPO Videotronic
Projector Corp.
222 East 44th Street
New York, New York 10017

Newcomb Audio Products Co.
12881 Bradley Avenue
Sylmar, California 91342

North American
Philips Corp. (Norelco)
Training and Education Systems
100 East 42nd Street
New York, New York 10017

Optisonics Corp.
Montgomeryville Industrial
Center
Montgomeryville, Pennsylvania 18036

Orrtronics Products Group
Faraday Inc.
805 South Maumee
Tecumseh, Michigan 49286

Paillard, Inc.
1900 Lower Road
Linden, New Jersey 07036

Panasonic, Matsushita
Electric Corp. of America
23-05 44th Street
Long Island City, New York 11101

Philips Broadcast
Equipment Corp.
1 Philips Parkway
Montvale, New Jersey 07645

Presentation Tech. Aids, Inc.
630 Ninth Avenue
New York, New York 10036

Programo, Inc.
44 West 44th
New York, New York 10036

Projection Optics Co.
271 11th Avenue
East Orange, New Jersey 07018

Quick Response Systems, Inc.
800 North West Street
Alexandria, Virginia 22314

Realist, Inc.
North 93 West
16288 Megal Drive
Menomenee Falls, Wisconsin 53051

Response Systems Corp.
Edgemont, Pennsylvania 19028

Retention Communications
Systems, Inc.
2 Pennsylvania Plaza
Suite 1199
New York, New York 10001

Revox Corp.
P.O. Box 196
Roslyn Heights, New York 11577

Rheem Califone
5922 Bowcroft Avenue
Los Angeles, California 90016

Sargent-Welch Scientific Co.
7300 North Linder Avenue
Skokie, Illinois 60076

Saunders Associates, Inc.
3 Old Boston Road
Wilton, Connecticut 06897

Scott Education Division
Holyoke, Massachusetts 01040

Self Development, Inc.
367 Almaden Avenue
San Jose, California 95110

Setchell Carlson Co.
SC Electronics, Inc.
Subsidiary Audiotronics Corp.
530 Fifth Avenue North West
Saint Paul, Minnesota 55112

Setco Audio-Visual, Inc.
4400 Saint Vincent Avenue
Webster Groves, Missouri 63119

Sharp Electronics Corp.
10 Keystone Place
Paramus, New Jersey 07652

Shibaden Corp. of America
58-25 Brooklyn Queens
Expressway
Woodside, New York 11377

Singer Co.
Simulation Products Division
Binghampton, New York 13902

Sony Corp. of America
VTR Division
47-47 Van Dam Street
Long Island City, New York 11101

Sony/Superscope, Inc.
8150 Vineland Avenue
Sun Valley, California 91352

Spindler and Sauppe, Inc.
1329 Grand Central Avenue
Glendale, California 91201

Standard Projector and
Equipment Co., Inc.
1911 Pickwick Avenue
Glenview, Illinois 60025

Synchronex Corp.
635 Madison Avenue
New York, New York 10022

Tandberg of America
8 Third Avenue
Pelham, New York 10803

Taylor Merchant Corp.
(T.M. Visual Industries, Inc.)
25 West 45th Street
New York, New York 10036

Teaching Dynamics, Inc.
Division Jetronics Industries, Inc.
Main and Cotton Streets
Philadelphia, Pennsylvania 19127

Teaching Technology Corp.
P.O. Box 3817
6837 Hayvenhurst Avenue
Van Nuys, California 91407

Technamation, Inc.
112 Parkway Drive South
Hauppauge, New York 11787

Technicolor, Inc.
Commercial and Educational
Division
299 Kalmus Drive
Costa Mesa, California 92627

Tel-A-Story, Inc.
517 Main Street
Davenport, Iowa 52805

Telepro Industries, Inc.
Cherry Hill Industrial Center
Cherry Hill, New Jersey 08034

Telex Communications Division
Telex-Magnecord-Viking
9600 Aldrich Avenue South
Minneapolis, Minnesota 55420

Triangle Projectors, Inc.
3706 Oakton Street
Skokie, Illinois 60076

University Microfilms
300 North Zeeb Road
Ann Arbor, Michigan 48106

Viewlex, Inc.
1 Broadway Avenue
Holbrook, New York 11741

Visual Educom, Inc.
4333 South Ohio Street
Michigan City, Indiana 46360

V M Corp.
P.O. Box 1247
Benton Harbor, Michigan 49022

White Electronics
Division Ltd.
3041 Universal Drive
Mississauga, Ontario, Canada

Whitehouse Products, Inc.
360 Furman Street
Brooklyn, New York 11201

Wilson Corporation
555 West Taft Drive
South Holland, Illinois 60473

Wollensak/3M Company
Building 224-6E,
3M Center
Saint Paul, Minnesota 55101

Zeiss Ikon
444 Fifth Avenue
New York, New York 10018

References

1. Bloom, B. *et al. Taxonomy of Educational Objectives, Handbook I: Cognitive Domain*, David McKay Company, Inc., New York, 1969.
2. Boucher B. *et al. Proceedings of Project ARISTOTLE Symposium, TASK Group II: Media,* National Security Industrial Association, Washington, D.C., 1967.
3. Bretz, R. *A Taxonomy of Communication Media,* Educational Technology Publications, Englewood Cliffs, New Jersey, 1971.
4. Bretz, R. *Selection of Appropriate Communication Media for Instruction, The: A Guide for Designers of Air Force Technical Training Programs,* The Rand Corporation, Santa Monica, California R-601-PR, 1971.
5. Brown, J. and Thornton, J., Jr. *New Media in Higher Education,* Association for Higher Education and the Division of Audiovisual Instructional Service of the National Education Association, Washington, D.C., 1963.
6. Dale, E. *Audio Visual Methods in Teaching,* The Dryden Press, Holt, Rinehart and Winston Inc., New York, 1969.
7. Davidson, R. *Audiovisual Machines,* International Textbook Company, Scranton, Pennsylvania, 1969.
8. Gagne, R. *et al. Psychological Principles in Systems Development,* Holt, Rinehart and Winston, Inc., New York, 1962.
9. Gerlach, V. and Ely, D. *Teaching and Media—A Systematic Approach,* Prentice-Hall, Inc., Englewood Cliffs, New Jersey, 1971.
10. Gronlund, N.E. *Stating Behavioral Objectives for Classroom Instruction,* Macmillan Company, New York, 1971.
11. Hericks, S., ed. *Audio Visual Equipment Directory, The, 18th Edition,* National Audio Visual Association, Inc., Fairfax, Virginia, 1972.
12. Hill, Joseph E. *The Educational Sciences 2nd ed.,* Oakland Community College Press, Bloomfield Hills, Michigan, 1968.
13. Jacobs, J. *An Evaluation of Programmed Instruction for Teaching Facts and Concepts,* Aerospace Medical Research Laboratories, Wright-Patterson Air Force Base, Ohio, AD631-414, 1965.
14. Mager, R. *Preparing Instructional Objectives,* Fearon Publishers, Lear Siegler, Inc., Belmont, California, 1962.
15. Mechner, F., Cook, D., and Margulies, S. *Introduction to Programmed Instruction,* Basic Systems, Inc., New York, 1964.
16. Rhode, W. *et al. Analysis and Approach to the Development of an Advanced Multimedia Instructional System,* Air Force Human Resources Laboratory, Wright-Patterson Air Force Base, Ohio AFHRL-TR-69-30, 1970.
17. Valverdez, H. *Maintenance Training Media—An Annotated Bibliography,* Aerospace Medical Research Laboratories, Wright-Patterson Air Force Base, Ohio, AMRL-TR-67-151, 1968.
18. Woodworth, R. and Schlosberg, H. *Experimental Psychology,* Holt, Rinehart and Winston, Inc., New York, 1962.
19. *Educational Product Report No. 39: Overhead Projectors*, Educational Products Information Exchange Institute, New York, 1971.

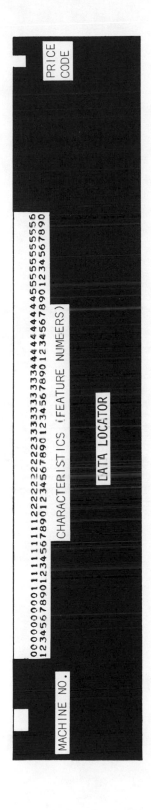

Figure 4

Data Locator Facsimile

NOTES

NOTES